Destiny Celibacy

Destiny Celibacy

Myth, truth, and tips for improvement of adult life in your best years.

BY

KURT GASSNER

My-mindguide.com

Destiny Celibacy
Kurt Gassner

Impressum
My-mindguide – The publishing trademarke of trendguide Capital GmbH, Klenzestr. 42a, 80469 Munich, Germany.

Reg. Nr. HRB Munich 206639, VAT 152 123 159, CEO: Kurt Friedrich Gassner
Web: www.my-mindguide.com, mail: gassner@my-mindguide.com

Paperback ISBN: 978-3-98793-920-4
Ebook ISBN: 978-3-949978-32-6
Hardback ISBN: 978-3-949978-31-9

Table of Contents

Forward

Ihave come across many older adults who complain about their declining sex life. One story that stood out to me was that of a seventy-five-year-old man in a seemingly perfect relationship.

Here is what he said to me:

"I'm happily married; I have three grown-up kids and a grandson. On the surface, I'm in a caring relationship. However, I'm unhappy.

The wild desire my wife and I had when we married disappeared years ago; she was never that much into sex. The decline started with a very regulated sex life that slowly became much reduced. Now there is no more romantic kissing—just a peck on the cheek—and sex has been reduced to a max of two times a month. My wife only allows it from the back with very sparse movement.

I don't blame my wife, but I still feel the glow under the surface. I still enjoy the swing of hips, glossy lips, and trying to catch a look from a beautiful woman. I think my wife knows, which is why she monitors my phone and gadgets and watches and registers every eye movement. So very often, she's jealous.

I love and respect my wife, but I want more. Am I a sick, dirty old man?"

The reality is that every man and woman experiences this as they age, although such frustrations are more common in males. Society isn't kind when it comes to older people and their sexuality. Older men are often called perverts when they complain about their sexuality and how they still want to have sex. Sexual-related disorders are underreported for both men and women. Sexual intimacy among older adults is a topic that is rarely discussed. According to specialists, the hush allows misunderstandings to develop, such as the widely held belief that elders lose interest in sex and are, or should be, asexual. Most young and even middle-aged people don't want to face the reality of becoming old since sex is associated with reproduction, youthful appearance, and power.

I belong to this age group, as I am currently undergoing the aging process, so I understand how you feel. My first thought about this book started when my friend had an issue.

After being frustrated by the whole situation, my friend, a sailor, decided to look for a younger attractive lady, who he's sailing the world with now. The price he had to pay for this is separation from his family and a strained relationship with his family and daughter, which he suffers to date because he chose a different path.

I also know many guys who use sports as an escape. They use a lot of extreme sports, activities, and noise to silence their inner emptiness. Some even take to drugging, drinking, and powerful meditation just to fill up this hole in their life.

As a self-improvement author who likes to empower his readers to better navigate the intricacies of life, I knew there had to be a better way to solve the issue of aging and intimacy. I began to ask questions and seek answers. I discovered epigenetics, social patterns, and the rules society has forced us to live by in my extensive search. I also dove deeper into medical science and social sciences.

The result? I found answers and solutions to help you understand and better your life. I aim to get you to live a life of pleasure with your spouse and help you change your life's current state.

Sometimes, it feels like a very comfortable prison. Is divorce separation the answer? Is there a way to change this natural hormone-based lack of desire? Is this blissful state of celibacy the answer?

As you begin to read this book, you will find answers to these and many more questions.

All I want is some
ice-cream, vodka and
an orgasm.
I'm simple
like that.

Introduction

Among men, sex sometimes results in intimacy; among women, intimacy sometimes results in sex.

—Barbara Cartland.

Most people believe that sex should not be much of a priority; however, many studies have shown that older people are still very active. An example of such a study is the 2017 survey by the University of Michigan that showed that 40 percent of people aged sixty-five to eighty are still sexually active.

Sex is a significant factor in ensuring a good quality of life for older adults. However, the reality is that problem can arise that makes sex difficult with aging. There is also the issue of reduced intimacy between both partners. Chronic medical conditions associated with aging also contribute to this problem.

As important as sex is to older adults, it is rarely addressed. A survey published by the *Journal of Clinical Gerontology and Geriatrics* shows that about 58 percent of doctors occasionally ask about their patient's sexual function and the rest never do. Now, compare this with the over 40 percent of older adults that are sexually active; there is a considerable gap.

Sexuality is part of our lives from a young age, and this doesn't change as we progress into old age. I find it highly unfair that older adults are seen as asexual and judged by society for simply trying to express their sexuality.

Older adults need to be supported in addressing this dimension in their human experience, which is my motivation for writing this book. In this book, we will be looking at the concept of sexuality and celibacy regarding older adults. I will also be sharing the critical thing you need to know about sex in old age. I'll cover the changes in sexual function and reveal some shocking truths. Here you will also find tips to address your sexuality.

People have always thought of sex as just vaginal intercourse, which is untrue; in this book, you will find other ways to have fulfilling sexual activity with your partner. I would also take us through the previous eras alongside communities in the twenty-first century to learn a thing or two and break the ageism in society.

One thing I'm sure of is that as you read and implement the things I will be showing you, you will begin to see changes in your sexual life—changes you never thought possible. My sincere advice is not to read this book like a novel. To see any active change in your life, take notes as you read along, set goals, decide what you want to implement (including when and how you will implement them). Don't rush to implement everything at once; take it slowly, one step at a time.

Your sexual health is in your hands. This book provides all the armor and ammunition to get you to your desired terminus.

Don't get shy about what society would say; speak up if you need to. Ensure you live your life to its fullest potential.

Evolution of Sex

Sex has always been an essential part of a couple's marital. It is, therefore, quite surprising that in the twenty-first century, sex amongst oldies is frowned upon and often not talked about. To fully understand this, let's take a look at how sex has evolved over the years.

But first, what we should look at is how sex was and is currently being expressed in various cultures.

- **India:** In India, the first evidence of attitudes towards sex in this region comes from the ancient texts of Hinduism, Buddhism, and Jainism. Sex was considered a mutual duty between a married couple where the husband and wife pleasured each other equally. (This was at least true of the followers.) There was polygamy, which was allowed in ancient times by rulers with many cultures or ruling classes practicing it. India is also known publicly for the *Kama Sutra*. This text was initially written for and kept by the philosophers, warriors, and nobles (along with their servants and concubine). The *Kama Sutra* details the way in which individuals should pleasure themselves. However, within the context of the Indian regions, sex was generally seen to be a moral duty of the partner in long-term marriages or relationships.

- **Japan:** The *Genji Monogatari*, popularly called the world's first novel, which goes as far back as the eighth century AD, talks about eroticism as the central part of the aesthetic life of the noble. The book's tone shows that sexuality was a valued component of cultured life—just as music or any of the arts is.

- **Ancient Greece:** In ancient Greece, the phallus was often used as an object of worship to symbolize fertility. This is usually expressed in Greek sculpture and other artwork. It was often believed that women envied the penises of males. Wives were often considered a commodity and tools for bearing children. Homosexuality and bisexuality were interwoven into the social institutions in Greece, such as education, art, religion, and politics. Ancient Greek men were big on prostitution and even believed it was necessary for pleasure.

- **Ancient Rome:** In ancient Rome, manliness was equated with the ability to control one's body, which was the concept of male sexuality. For women, their sexual integrity was displayed through their displayed attractiveness and self-control. Women were encouraged to express their sexuality. Art was also a central medium for the depiction of sexuality in these times. Sexual positions and scenarios were shown in wall murals, for instance.

In the eighteenth century, marital sex was commonly referred to as "sharing a bed" and seen as very important—so vital that it was denoted to show reconciliation and forgiveness. Many men said that having sex was evidence that they had been forgiven of their transgressions. "Not sharing a bed" was then used to indicate the breakdown of the marriage or relationship.

In this time, marital intimacy was shown by touching and caressing. This intimacy involved walking together arm-in-arm, stroking, caressing, embracing, flirting, spending time together alone, and exchanging gifts.

These couples also engaged in several sexual positions, the man on top being the most common position but only one of myriad possibilities.

The number of children the couples had throughout their lives indicated that the couples kept having sex as they aged.

In these times, wives were expected to be sexually welcoming to their husbands. The sex was also expected to be enjoyable. There was evidence of women's enjoyment as seen by their willingness to engage in extramarital affairs. The first half of the eighteenth century had common descriptions of sexually-assertive women.

A good example can be found in 1719. Simeon Bardou, when testifying against his mistress, noted she: ". . . embraced me in her arms and took my hand and put it on her naked belly and told me that she could give me no plainer demonstration of her love than allowing me all the freedom I could desire . . . I was prevailed upon to have carnal dealings with her" and "She often came there to me; yea, she came so frequently that I caused deny myself to her."

Sex was so crucial that marriage annulments could occur on account of male impotence.

However, later in the century, new models of chastity began to change and affect both the understanding of female sexual behavior as well as women's enjoyment of sex. Women were now described in a passive manner, even in cases of adultery. Now women were just not seen as sexually passive, but the adoption of these ideas began to affect a woman's sexual behavior to a significant extent. This increasing expectancy of chastity influenced not just the social attitudes but also the marital bed.

In this twenty-first century, the perception of sex has again changed. *Prima* magazine carried out a study that focused on how women's attitudes towards love, sex, and marriage had shifted since the 1940s. They discovered that married women have less sex today than their grandmothers did. In the 1950s, women had sex about two times a week; however, two-thirds of today's women said they were too tired to manage that much.

The *Prima* study found that sex before marriage was now the norm, and it tends to die down after marriage.

Most women are saddled with the responsibility of working, taking care of the home, and looking after the kids, so when they go to bed, they are too tired to do anything but sleep.

Older women are more open to the idea of sex since the family roles are over.

Some of these sexual changes that come with aging can be positive for older women. They have already learned what excites them and are more inclined to share it with younger and less experienced partners. An older woman's sexual experience can also transform into body confidence and sexual prowess. Plus, with less chance of unwanted pregnancy, many older women can now enjoy sex freely.

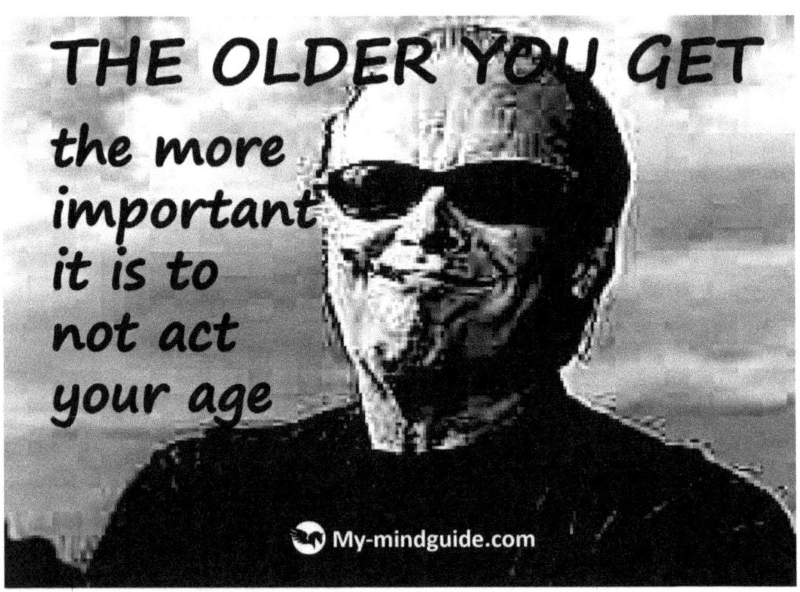

THE OLDER YOU GET
the more important it is to not act your age
My-mindguide.com

Chapter 1

The Concept of Sexuality

Sexuality and the desire for intimacy are essential for a good quality of life from birth until death. It is a means of expressing love and care to the partner. Sexuality may include caressing, touching, fantasy, masturbation, physical closeness, and warmth. By sustaining and strengthening the ability of older people to continue their sexual needs, there is a significant improvement in their quality of life.

The sexuality of older people in society is described as inappropriate, bizarre, or obscene. Only negative thoughts pop into their heads when people think of older adults and sex. Older adults are commonly thought of as either:

- "Cute" in a childlike and chaste way,
- Predatory, as in a "cougar" or a "dirty old man," or
- Problematic

These thoughts arise and are labeled based on if and how they choose to express their sexuality or not. The truth, however, is that these labels are very different from reality. Intimacy and healthy sex life are essential for a good older life.

Most people think it is natural that a person's sex life should decline with increasing age. However, this isn't true. What is true is that, over time, aging tends to change the way the body and the mind function, significantly affecting sexuality.

The good news is that these changes don't necessarily imply that sex should stop at a certain point or age; what it means is that you need to make specific adaptations to accommodate your and your partner's changing bodies and needs.

There are hormonal and psychological changes associated with aging that affect sexual interest. Understanding these changes and how they affect you and your partner will significantly improve your sexual life.

Let's look at the regular age-related changes in men and women.

Physiologic Changes in Women
With aging, there is a decline in sexual activity for females from 40 percent in women of ages 65–74 to less than 20 percent in those 75–85.

In women, the most predominant change that affects sexuality is menopause. Menopause usually occurs at about age fifty in most women, and it has associated reductions in estrogen, progesterone, and androgen levels. Reduction in these hormones causes changes to the vagina, which can then lead to challenges:

- Reduction in pubic hair
- Decrease in the vagina secretion

- Thinning of the vaginal wall and vulva
- Increase in vaginal pH

These changes in the genitals then cause a difference in the sex response cycle of the females. So, as a result, they experience:

- Delayed excitement and orgasm
- Postcoital bleeding
- Mild burning sensations during intercourse
- Painful intercourse

Physiologic Changes in Men

Despite aging, men generally retain more desire for and interest in sex than their female counterparts—70 percent of men over seventy report that they are still very interested in sexual activity. Regardless of the sustained interest in sex, some changes can impact the quality of sex they experience.

With age, there is a decrease in the testosterone levels, scrotal vasocongestion, and reduced tensing of the scrotal sac, which results in

- Delayed aroused
- Longer refractory periods after an orgasm before having sex again

Erectile dysfunction is also a significant result of aging in men. It is estimated that 55 percent of men experience impotence by age seventy-five. Aside from the natural decrease in the body's testosterone production, certain medications used to treat aging-related conditions can also further reduce this level and cause sexual difficulties for you.

Below is a list of some medications that can cause or contribute to your sexual difficulty.

- Pain medications such as opiates (e.g., morphine and hydromorphone)
- High blood pressure medications such as thiazide diuretics, beta-blockers, and spironolactone
- Enlarged prostate medication such as finasteride
- Prostate cancer medications such as anti-androgens and other testosterone blockers
- Depression, anxiety, and other mood medications
- Atrial fibrillation medications such as digoxin
- Stomach ulcer medications

Debunking Myths About Aging and Sexuality

MYTH 1: *Sexuality is not for older people*
Fact: Sexuality is for everyone irrespective of age. It contributes to healthy aging by promoting physical, mental, and social well-being. This adds to a good quality of life and a sense of self-worth.

MYTH 2: *Only younger people are sexually active*
Fact: Older people can be sexy. A 1999 survey conducted by AARP and *Modern Maturity Magazine* found that the percentage of people aged forty-five and above who consider their partners physically attractive increases with age.

MYTH 3: *Sexuality is only about sex*
Fact: Sexuality is expressed in many different ways. It means different things to other people. It includes looking and feeling

good, companionship, emotional connection with your partner, romantic and emotional intimacy, and sex.

MYTH 4: *After a certain age, men and women are unable to perform sexually*

Fact: You can still have a delightful and satisfying sex life. Although some physical changes are unavoidable, it doesn't imply that you would have irrevocable sexual problems. With the use of medications, both men and women can treat sexual dysfunction and remain sexually active. A study showed that 61 percent of people over 60 years said their sex life was the same or better than in their forties, and 26 percent of people over 75 said they remained sexually active.

MYTH 5: *Older adults shouldn't be worried about STDs*

Fact: There is an increasing infection rate of STDs such as gonorrhea and syphilis among older adults. With age, the weakening of the immune system makes them more susceptible to these infections, so it's essential to take the necessary precautionary steps.

Intimacy Is Not Just Sex.

When we think of intimacy, all we think about is sex. Many believe that the two terms are synonymous; however, this is not so. We tend to assume that the closest we can possibly get physically to another human is through sex; however, at least four types of intimacy don't involve sex at all but are very important to a romantic relationship.

As you and your partner grow older, you must incorporate these other forms of intimacy that I will be showing you. They help foster rapport and chemistry and even promote better physical intimacy. These types of intimacy include:

1. Emotional Intimacy: Emotional intimacy simply means that both you and your partner are comfortable and feel at ease about expressing your emotions with each other. Generally, we tend to confide in those we trust because we know they wouldn't belittle or embarrass us. So emotional intimacy between you and your partner involves sharing thoughts and feelings, telling each other your dreams, disappointments, fears, and feeling understood when you do share. You both feel this safe space is cultivated when there is no judgment or contempt when the other party decides to share their emotions. An example of emotional intimacy is a woman telling her husband that she's unhappy about her body after having a baby. She trusts that her spouse will offer her comfort and help her to draw up solutions to the situation, not to be dismissive about her feelings. You can increase emotional intimacy by having a more profound and reflective conversation about emotions and experiences you wouldn't usually share with others. Ask thoughtful questions and always focus on listening to understand rather than listening to respond. It is essential that you are careful not to invalidate their feelings, as this can shut the door to future conversation.

2. Intellectual Intimacy: Intellectual intimacy means that both of you in the relationship are able to think freely. Your beliefs and opinions are valued, and you are comfortable communicating your view and viewpoints without being worried about potential disagreements. There is no pressure

to agree, and the atmosphere allows for a stimulating conversation that helps you become closer to your partner. An example of intellectual intimacy is when a couple reads and discusses a book together. The two of them compare their opinions on it, not disagreeing with each other's thoughts. You can increase emotional intimacy with your partner by making a conscious effort to have these talks without becoming angry or defensive. This type of intimacy aims to connect through logic and expression.

3. Experimental Intimacy: Experimental intimacy establishes a feeling of closeness and bonding through the inside jokes and private memories you and your partner share. Here you act as a team and move in unison with the aim of achieving a common goal while creating an experience. Examples of experimental intimacy include: cooking a meal with your partner or visiting a city both of you have never been to, so you'll experience it for the first time together. You can increase experimental intimacy with your partner by taking on new adventures and planning activities that neither of you has done before.

4. Spiritual Intimacy: Now, this doesn't refer to religious practice. It refers to the closeness you and your partner form when you share poignant memories. Praying and worshiping as a couple can qualify as such memories; however, that is not the only example. Other examples include watching the sunrise or sunset together, taking a walk while holding hands, reading a couple of passages from your religious text together before bed every night. You can increase spiritual intimacy by talking with your partner about spirituality and

discovering experiences that each of you considers inspiring, and doing those activities together.

How intimate are you and your partner?

Intimacy should be natural in a loving relationship. As you and your partner grow older, it may be challenging to maintain closeness and healthy sex life. Keeping the intimacy in your relationship helps you reinforce your physical and emotional bond with your partner.

Today, the media tries to perpetuate the idea of "perfect sex," which can leave you wondering what you may be missing out on. However, there is no such thing as perfect sex. How you express intimacy is personal and unique to each couple. You need to discover what works for you and what doesn't.

There are so many reasons why intimacy may be lost. Some of these reasons include:

- Use of drugs: Just like we've covered above, certain drugs that treat age-related disorders cause problems with intimacy; these issues include erectile dysfunction or a reduced sex drive.

- Disorders: With aging come various conditions that can interfere with physical intimacy. Diabetes and vascular disorders can lead to erectile dysfunction; arthritis can limit and make movements painful. The pain, discomfort, worry, and drugs associated with each disease reduce the desire for intimacy. For your partner, they can also face reduced intimacy due to the stress and demands of caregiving.

- Loss or absence of a partner is a significant barrier to intimacy.

- Low levels of sex hormones, as I mentioned earlier, cause changes that make the process of sex painful, uncomfortable, and challenging. There is also the possibility of having a decreased sex drive.

- Differences in the expectations of you and your partner. You might want certain expressions of intimacy, and your partner might not.

- Older people are reluctant to discuss the problems that affect their intimacy. They can feel embarrassed about the changes in their body (e.g., wrinkles, sagging flesh, etc.).

- Older people who live in a residential care facility or with family members don't have as much privacy, affecting their intimacy.

- Some illnesses, disabilities, and surgeries can also cause sexual problems and affect you and your partner's intimacy.

- Arthritis: Arthritis can cause severe joint pain that can make sexual contact very uncomfortable. Exercise, drugs, and in some cases joint replacement surgery may help relieve this pain. Also, take warm baths and rest as much. One major disadvantage of this condition is that you cannot engage in early morning sex as the joint pain is worse in the morning. So planning the timing of your sexual activity can be very beneficial.

- Chronic pain: Pain interferes while we age, and intimacy is not spared. Luckily, you don't have to experience unending chronic pain since it can be treated. The downside to this treatment is that some of these medications interfere with sexual function, so don't hesitate to talk to your doctor if you notice any side effects.

- Dementia: Dementia is a neurologic disease that affects older people. Some studies have shown that some people with dementia show an increased interest in sex, intimacy, and physical closeness. However, they may not be able to judge what is appropriate sexual behavior. Because they may be unable to recognize their spouse or partner and they still desire sexual contact, they may seek it with someone else. If you are caught in this situation, it can be difficult to know how to handle it so talk to a doctor. nurse, or social worker, which may be helpful.

- Diabetes: Diabetes is a disease that occurs as a result of high blood glucose. It is one of the illnesses that can cause erectile dysfunction in some men. Medical treatment can help in most cases. There isn't a lot of research regarding how diabetes affects older women's sexuality, but women with diabetes are more likely to have a vaginal yeast infection, which can cause itching and irritation, making sex uncomfortable and undesirable. Yeast infections can be treated.

- Heart disease: Heart disease results from the narrowing and hardening of the arteries. This changes the blood vessels and stops blood from flowing freely. The result of this is that men and women may find it more difficult to orgasm. For both men and women, it may take longer to become aroused, and for men, it may be more difficult to get and maintain an erection. People that have had a heart attack (and their partners) may worry that sex could cause another heart attack. Sexual activity is generally safe; however, it is necessary that you always follow your doctor's advice. Discuss your options with your doctors and always monitor changes in your heart.

- Incontinence: Incontinence refers to loss of bladder control or could mean leaking of urine. It is more common in older adults, especially women. During sex, extra pressure on the belly can cause urine to leak. Incontinence can be helped by changing positions or emptying the bladder before and after sex. Incontinence can be treated, so speak to your physician about it.

- Stroke: This is a neurological condition in which one-half of the body suffers paralysis. Stoke can affect one's ability to have sex. By changing positions or using medical devices, people with paralysis or weakness can still have sex. Even people with paralysis from the waist down can still experience pleasure and orgasm.

- Depression: Depression can manifest itself as a lack of interest in activities you previously enjoyed such as intimacy and sexual activity. It's not always easy to tell whether you're depressed. Consult your physician. Depression is treatable.

- Surgery. Many of us are apprehensive about undergoing any type of surgery, and it's much more difficult when it involves the breasts or the genital area. Most people return to the type of sex life they had before to surgery. There are certain surgeries that involve the reproductive or sexual organs.

o *Hysterectomy* is a surgery to remove a woman's uterus for a variety of reasons, including discomfort, bleeding, fibroids, and other complications. When an older woman gets a hysterectomy, her ovaries are removed as well. When it comes to deciding whether or not to get this surgery, both women and their partners may be concerned about their future sexual lives. If you're concerned about any changes you might experience with a hysterectomy, talk with your gynecologist or surgeon.

o *Mastectomy* is a procedure in which all or part of a woman's breast is removed due to breast cancer. Some women may lose their sexual interest as a result of the surgery, or they may feel less desirable or appealing to their partners. In addition to speaking with your doctor, it may be beneficial to speak with other women who have undergone this procedure. Consult your cancer doctor or surgeon if you want your breast reconstructed.

o *Prostatectomy* is a procedure in which all or part of a man's prostate is removed due to cancer or an enlarged prostate. It has the potential to induce urinary incontinence or ED. If you require this procedure, discuss your concerns with your doctor prior to surgery.

- Medications: Some medicines might lead to sexual issues. Some blood pressure medications, antihistamines, antidepressants, tranquilizers, Parkinson's disease or cancer meds, appetite suppressants, mental health treatments, and ulcer medications are among them. Some of these might cause ED or make it difficult for men to ejaculate. Some medicines can lower a woman's sexual desire, create vaginal dryness, or make arousal and orgasm harder. Consult your doctor to check if there is a medication that doesn't have this side effect.

- Alcohol: Alcohol abuse can lead to erectile issues in males and a delay in orgasm in women.

Below is a quiz that will help you identify where the problem may be coming from, your emotional triggers, and what you and your partner should do to rectify these discrepancies.

I recommend that you and your partner take this test independently. Being around each other may influence your answers and affect your ability to accurately picture things.

Q1. When I think about my sex life, I feel . . .
a. It's good enough, but I don't have time to worry about it too much
b. I'm not happy with the sex in my relationship, but I can't express that
c. Worried that my friends and everyone else have more and better sex than me
d. I don't have sex very often, and that works for both of us most of the time

e. I have a satisfying sex life that works for my partner and me

Q2. For me, sex is really . . .
a. Something I try to get out of whenever possible
b. Something I don't have in my relationship
c. A way of elevating our relationship above just being "housemates."
d. satisfaction and pleasure
e. Intimacy and connection to my partner

Q3. When I think about ways of boosting the intimacy in our relationship . . .
a. I don't think it's possible—our sex life is what it is
b. I don't know how to talk to my partner about it
c. I'd appreciate some tips and techniques, but I'm not sure where to start
d. I try to talk to my partner about what I'd like, but sometimes I get a bit embarrassed
e. We enjoy coming up with new things to try

Q4. When it comes to sex, my partner . . .
a. Isn't interested and won't talk to me about it
b. Gets annoyed and has sex reluctantly
c. Is too busy, and there are too many pressures on our time to prioritize it
d. Is usually happy to have sex
e. It makes time for us to be intimate

Q5. When we have sex, I feel . . .
a. Bored and disconnected from my partner
b. It's more for my partner than for me

c. Under pressure to perform and tend to just go through the motions

d. It's enjoyable, but I want to try new things

e. I emotionally connected to my partner, and we have fun

Q6. The biggest obstacle to our sex life is . . .
a. I just can't be bothered, and it's a shallow priority
b. My partner makes excuses a lot of the time that s/he's not in the mood
c. We hardly have any privacy in our home
d. We usually make an effort and create the space to be together

Q7. When it comes to broaching the subject of sex in our relationship, I . . .
a. Change the subject and clam up
b. Get irritated that my partner is bothering me with this topic again
c. Want to work things out, but we just end up arguing
d. Feel that we try to make it a priority to talk but get distracted by other worries
e. Feel we talk a lot, and it keeps us close and connected

Q8. When it comes to expressing other ways of being intimate, my partner and I . . .
a. Don't do anything
b. Have mechanical sex, and that's enough
c. Tell each other that we love each additional
d. Try to get into the habit of having regular hugs/physical contact
e. Tend to hold hands, talk, laugh, and cuddle often

When i get old i don't want people thinking "What a sweet little old lady";; I want 'em saying"Oh Crap! What's she up to now?"
My-mindguide.com

Chapter 2

Celibacy

Celibacy simply refers to the practice of not having sex. Although the idea is the same, people practice different ways of being celibate. Some abstain from all kinds of sexual contact, including kissing or holding hands while others refrain from sexual intercourse.

Sometimes this act of celibacy can be unplanned and it occurs when someone doesn't have sex for months or years without intending to

Are Older People Being Forced into a Life of Celibacy?
For us to understand this, I want us to look at this study.

According to the poll, about a third of all males over the age of fifty—and nearly a quarter of those who live with their spouses and partners—do not have sexual intercourse. Mori's study of 802 men found that a significant percentage of elderly British men suffered from prostate difficulties, which made them irritated and worried.

According to the poll, sexually active males had a high level of fidelity, with 79 percent of 50–59-year-olds having only had intercourse with one woman in the preceding year. Only 5 percent of respondents said they had sex with more than one lady.

In the preceding year, 45 percent of sexually active people claimed they had a sexual issue, the most prevalent of which was a weak erection.

Dr. Andrew Stanway, a psycho-sexual medicine specialist who assisted in the study's design, was astounded by the lack of sexual engagement in such a big percentage of older males. Other polls indicated significantly greater levels of activity. "Overall, 31 percent of males over the age of fifty stated they were not having any sex at all," according to Dr. Stanway, including 23 percent of men with spouses or partners.

Only a few guys admitted to having attempted anything other than penetrative sexual contact. Oral sex was the only other sexual activity that a substantial percentage of people engaged in (20 percent).

Moreover, over half of the males (56 percent) stated they no longer masturbated, while 9 percent indicated they had never done so before.

Men also reported that sex grew less pleasurable as they got older, according to the findings. The poll was aimed at finding out how many men had prostate issues—and if there was a relationship—as well as measuring levels of sexual engagement.

When given a list of symptoms, 45 percent of the males reported they had one or more of them. Sufferers were more likely to have a less active sex life, be apprehensive, and feel down.

Currently, there is a decrease in the rate of global mortality alongside an aging generation of baby boomers. This means that the current demographic of older adults is currently increasing alongside the scope of their sex lives.

Research has shown that lifelong sexual function is an essential factor in achieving successful aging. Despite this, older adults face a lot of social and self-stigma, the perpetuation of sexual myths and misinformation, and the lack of STI prevention programs.

The Partner Gap

The partner gap is something we should also look into. The physical changes that occur with age give people another chance to renew and restart their lovemaking by causing them to focus on intimacy and closeness in other ways. Because there is less focus on performance, there is room for affection and closeness to be expressed through acts such as cuddling, kissing, and stroking.

There is less compulsion to have as much sex as we age, but the freedom from necessity offers an excellent chance for couples to reconnect. Sex then becomes a matter of choice and, therefore, more exciting and intriguing to both parties.

However, among older women—widowed, divorced, or single—getting a partner may be difficult.

This partner gap largely inhibits women's social and sexual activity as they attain older ages. Older men are seen to be more likely than older women to be married and have sex partners.

According to many reports, women make up the bulk of the elderly without spouses. This is because women live longer than males, and healthy older men prefer to date younger women. Society also considers older women to be less beautiful than their male counterparts, a double standard that women's organizations have long criticized.

Older Adults and Other Forms of Relationships

Older adults are constantly finding new ways to express their sexuality. One such way is BDSM. The famous saying "you're only as old as you feel" simply lets you know that you shouldn't give up on trying new things no matter what age you are. BDSM isn't for everyone, but it may be just what you're looking for. While it can be physical, it can also be exciting, sensual, and even therapeutic without touching or being touched by another person.

The most popular kink among the over-sixties, according to research, was BDSM. In fact, 63 percent of those polled said that they would like to try it out with their spouse.

The survey also discovered that age play, a type of roleplaying in which people treat each other as if they are younger or older, is a popular pastime among the elderly. Sixty percent of those polled cexpressed an interest in trying it out.

Surprisingly, 58 percent of over-sixties stated they were interested in group sex with two or more additional individuals, making it the third most popular kink. This was closely followed by dominating and submissive sex (which piqued the curiosity of 56 percent of the age group) and scene roleplaying (which piqued the interest of 53 percent of respondents).

I'll be showing you what BDSM is and how it can benefit older people and how you can get started.

BDSM is an acronym that stands for bondage/discipline/sadism/masochism. It can also mean bondage/discipline/slave/master (or mistress). It generally covers things like fetish play, gender play, age play, where someone assumes an age that is not their chronological age (not involving underage individuals), and so much more.

It's very possible that you have had an unusual erotic interest for a long time but have been too afraid to try it; now is the time to experience all this community has in store.

The BDSM practice is guided by a principle called safe, sane, and consensual (SSC)—*safe* because the most vital parts of BDSM play are emotional and physical safety, *sane* because BDSM activities should be approached with a clear, rational head (including an understanding that not all fantasies can or should be acted out), and finally, *consensual* because permission to do anything must be politely requested, clearly given by parties who are all fully capable of doing so, and with the mutual understanding that consent can be withdrawn at any time and must be respected without repercussions.

It's essential to gain as much knowledge as possible before engaging in actual action. You can learn by reading well-respected how-to books, taking online or in-person workshops, or seeing or receiving hands-on technique demonstrations from BDSM educators. After all, the BDSM community places a strong emphasis on and encourages learning.

A vital aspect of any BDSM play is good communication: being able to talk freely and have your thoughts heard and respected and having things come to an abrupt conclusion if any of this stops—should be a fundamental part of every scene.

Part of this is accomplished by using a safeword, which is a pre-agreed word or phrase that, when used, causes everything to slow down, stop, or entirely stop. Some individuals use the traffic light system—*green, amber,* and *red*—instead of a specific safeword: *green* meaning "I love this; keep going," *amber* meaning "I'm a bit unsure; slow down," and *red* meaning "stop everything right now!"

How Does BDSM Benefit You?

There are two benefits to the process: physical benefits and emotional benefits. On the surface, BDSM may appear to be scary; however, the truth is that kink is what you want it to be, including gentle and soothing.

Physical Benefits: BDSM can become a satisfying coping mechanism when the play is adjusted to fit the health conditions you may have. Play is usually adjusted to accommodate any movement difficulties, joint pain, and cardiovascular concerns you may have. For example, gentle flogging on the shoulders can be an effective massage. By knowing your body and trying out different kinds of play, you'll be able to arrive at that which is enjoyable for you.

Emotional Benefits: As I mentioned earlier, BDSM isn't limited to whips, chains, and other things like that. Roleplay is another side of BDSM—referred to as the emotional side. Roleplay involves putting together a fun and fulfilling experience for everyone. Now you and your partner can decide on the kind of scenes you want to have, such as positive, supportive, and kind commands. It's okay to allow your imagination and passions to run wild when it comes to finding potentially rewarding roles. While fiction often does a poor job of representing physical play, it may occasionally serve as a tremendous source of inspiration for domination and submission scenarios.

Just remember that anything you want to do is never unusual, weird, or perverse as long as it's safe, sane, and consensual: if it gets you aroused, comfortable, and joyful, then go for it!

Sexual Expression in Old age Sometimes Transitions to Collecting Erotic Art

In the 2004 movie *Meet the Fockers*, which starred Robert De Niro, Barbara Streisand, Dustin Hoffman, and others, there were scenes where pieces of erotic art were all over the house—paintings, sculptures, and all kinds of things. With the understanding of the full spectrum of sexuality, the movie allowed us to see the sexual expression of the Fockers family. Both the husband and the wife had an intense appreciation for erotic art, and it allowed them to become better lovers even at their age. The freedom it gave them and their marriage was incredible, which rubbed off on others in the movie.

For some older people, the collection of erotic art and items are disassociated with pornography. Many people find it strange that older people keep erotic art in their homes; some label them porn addicts. This stereotype has made much older generations feel queer about their fascination with that kind of art. On the contrary, erotic art and pornography are two different things; while pornography creates an illusion of what sex is, erotic art is purely a matter of aesthetics and beauty.

Many older generations will become addicts of erotic art because it helps them express themselves; it gives them liberation to be able to express who they are freely. After all, our Sexuality is a part of us; what we feel, think, and do are all part of our makeup. As people grow old, the ability to have sex as often as they would like to might dwindle because of the issues that we have raised, but the appreciation for their sexual fantasies and tendencies can be satisfied through art. The same way artists use their paintings and sculptures to escape is more or less what the older generation uses the art for. It provides a perfect escape from the stereotype that older generations aren't allowed to be sexually active.

Being sexually active encompasses much more than intercourse. It also involves the feelings, thoughts, and behaviors that showcase deep affection for someone.

It is safe to say that the older generation is looking for an escape—a chance to feel what they once felt before—and for this reason, the collection of erotic art, watches, and other items helps them to fill that void.

How Does the Sex Drive Change Over the Years?

The sex drive is influenced by a lot of factors, including psychological, social, and physical dynamics, with hormones playing the most significant role. Throughout our lifetime, the factors combine differently and become modified to influence our sex drive. Let's take a look at what happens at different ages.

Your Twenties

- Men: The testosterone hormone needed for sexual arousal is very high at this age. In your twenties, you can also be anxious about sex because you're inexperienced.

- Women: women tend to be more fertile from their teen years and into their late twenties. So, they become pickier about if and when they have sex. Researchers also believe that the female desire might go up just as fertility begins to reduce toward the end of the twenties.

Your Thirties and Early Forties

- Men: Most men at this age have a strong sex drive, although testosterone levels begin to decline around age thirty-five. It is said to go down by 1 percent every year. However, it is faster in some men. The stress of work, family, and other commitments also influences how interested you are in sex at this period.

- Women: At this time, the sex drive is the strongest. A study showed that women between ages twenty-seven and forty-five have stronger sexual fantasies than younger or older women. They also had more sex.

- Women having kids changes things. Pregnancy and childbirth have a significant impact on sex life at any age. The body and hormones change throughout the pregnancy phase. There's a usual boost or increase in libido during the second trimester and a decreased desire for the other sex at other times. Breastfeeding, raising kids, and other work can significantly impact the time, energy, and interest you may have in sex.

Your Fifties and Beyond

- Men: With good physical and mental health, most men tend to continue to enjoy sex as they grow older. However, there is an increased likelihood of getting ED. Your erections may happen less and may not be as hard. Other health issues that occur with age, such as diabetes, high cholesterol level, heart disease, obesity, and even drug that treat these conditions, can cause a reduction in the sex drive.

- Women: Around this age, there is less worry about getting pregnant, which can make some women more interested in sex. Women tend to attain menopause around this age, which leads to a drop in estrogen levels, reducing the sex drive. There is also an associated vaginal dryness. Symptoms of menopause such as hot flashes, anxiety, weight gain, and sleep problems can also result in lower sex drive.

How the Ageist and Sexist Expectations of Society Affect Sexual Drive

In addition, the cultural expectations of gendered homosexuality are that men are made to look more sexually assertive while women are sexually passive. This stereotype also influences how men and women understand each other sexually, furthermore affecting how married couples experience sex, and it can often result in marital conflict.

Heterosexuality plays an important role in defining manhood and womanhood in our culture today. Our cultural ideas about gender are interwoven, and they rely heavily on sexuality. Even our understanding of heterosexuality is rooted in gender meaning and sustaining a gender hierarchy.

The whole idea of heterosexuality rests on an image of youthful bodies, driven by uncontrollable levels of penis-driven sexual desire. Most men are unable to match their desire level with this expected image, and as they age, it becomes increasingly difficult to keep up. Men over fifty experience a sharp decline in levels of sexual desire, which can cause them to question their ability to be appropriately "masculine." This, in turn, will often compel them to take Viagra to deal with their ED in a bid to realign their sexual experiences with the masculinity expectations of society.

Women aren't left out. The cultural expectations of feminine sexuality are rooted in women's sexual passivity. Women are expected to be receptive and desirable to men. This expected sexual desirability refers to society's standards of youthful beauty and attractiveness that consider older women and their bodies unattractive.

Now, both men and women fear getting old, but women particularly fear looking old because of this notion that aging women are unattractive. This mix of the ageist and sexist constructions that women have to face can explain why aging affects women earlier and more adversely than men. These bodily changes may lessen a woman's ability to conform to these expectations of feminine sexuality and therefore lower her interest in sex.

What Patterns Can We Consider?

There's a popular stereotype that men will "do it at any time," but women would "do it" only if the candles are scented right or if the partner has done the dishes first. Funny right? But is it true? Do men really have a stronger sex drive than women? Let's take a look.

There are some differences; however, it's not a clear-cut situation. Studies have shown that men's sex drives are not only stronger than women's but much more straightforward. Women place more value on emotional connection as a determinate of sexual desire. Moreover, social and cultural factors also influence them. So, the sources of women's sex drive are much harder to pin down. There are patterns we can look into that can give us more insight into the sex drives of men and women.

- Men think more about sex: Most men under the age of sixty think about sex at least once a day. Only about one-quarter of women think about sex as frequently as men. With age, men fantasize about it twice as much while females fantasize about it less. Roy Baumeister, a social psychologist at Florida State University, discovered that males reported higher spontaneous sexual arousal and had more frequent and diverse fantasies compared to research comparing male and female sex drives.

- Men look for sex more avidly: Men want more times than women at the beginning of a relationship, in the middle of it, and even many years after the start of the relationship. This is also true not only amongst heterosexuals but also homosexuals. Gay couples are seen to have sex more often than lesbians at all stages of their relationship. Men are also more open to the idea of a lot of sex partners in their lifetime and are open to the idea of casual sex. Even if sex is outlawed, men are more likely to seek it. An example of this is masturbation. About two-thirds of men say they masturbate even though they feel guilty about it, while amongst women, the frequency of masturbation is smaller. Another example is that nuns are better at keeping their chastity vows than priests. A survey carried out on several clergypersons saw 62 percent of priests agreeing to sexual activity compared to 42 percent of nuns.

- The things that excite women are more complicated than that of men: A very common question we hear is "what turns a woman on?" Shockingly, not even women seem to know what turns them on. Men are usually very specific and rigid about who they are aroused by, who they want to have sex with, and even who they fall in love with. On the other hand, this isn't so for women. For example, women are more open to the idea of homosexuality than men are because of their less-directed sex drives.

- Social and cultural factors influence women's sex drives: Religion is a perfect example of this. Women who regularly attend church are more likely not to have permissive views about sex. On the other hand, men don't show a connection between attending church and sexual attitudes. Women's attitudes and willingness to be involved in sexual activities are influenced by the environment more than men. The attitudes of their peers also influence women in decisions regarding sex. Also, women with a higher education level are more open to a wider variety of sexual practices, but education didn't make much of a difference with men. So generally, women are seen to show inconsistency between their expression of sexual activities (e.g., premarital sex and their actual behavior). The reason that it seems that women's sex drive can be easily influenced can be linked to the greater power men have in society alongside the different sexual expectations of men.

- The route to sexual satisfaction in women isn't direct: Women take a different path than men to arrive at sexual desire. For women, it's more about the anticipation than the destination, the longing that fuels the passion. Women utilize a lot of imagination and require connection and love in a relationship, which all influence the sexual drive. Men don't need as much imagination because the process is more straightforward for them. For men, sex is usually the connection, while women tend to talk first, connect first and then have sex. So women express their intimacy through the bond they form first and then sex, but for men, sex is the way they express intimacy.

- Women experience orgasms differently: Men take about four minutes to get an orgasm, but women usually take about ten to eleven minutes to reach orgasm (if they actually do). Another thing to note is how often the two sexes have orgasms during sex. Most times, men strain orgasms more often than women do.

- Women's libido experience is often reduced in response to drugs: since men's sex drive is closely linked with biology and directed, unlike that of women, it is easier for a low sex drive to be treated through medication in men. So, drugs are available for men for issues like erectile dysfunction as well as a shrinking libido. However, with women, there's no particular drug that's available that can boost their sex drive. Testosterone has actually been linked to affecting the sex drive of both men and women; however, it works a lot faster in men with low libidos than in women. Treatments generally aren't as effective in women as they are in men.

Involuntary Celibacy

As people age, their sexual relationship may die off such that one partner may want sex and the other may not. This causes an "ongoing involuntary celibacy" for the partner that wants sex. Many long-term marriages end up in this unhappy state.

Both genders are involved in this. There's an ongoing stereotype that men end up involuntarily celibate; however, there has been an increase in involuntarily celibate females over the years.

Although the types vary differently from couple to couple, there are four main types.

1. Slowed over time: This category is experienced by so many couples. The couple usually starts sexually active, which

diminishes over time. They typically are unable to identify when or why they stopped sex completely.

2. Stopped abruptly: The couples started sexually active but abruptly stopped due to events like pregnancy, illness, and infidelity.

3. Little sexual activity ever: Here, the couples report that from the very beginning, sex was always tricky. The team stated that the experience was never really rewarding for either of them. It can be related to sexual dysfunction, trauma, inhibition, shame, etc.

4. No clear pattern: Here, there are so many starts and stops at different times in the marriage for one reason or another.

Sex After Celibacy: How to Manage the Side Effects?

Have you taken a break from sex due to your age, health issues, or not having a partner? Whatever the reason is for your celibacy, whether it has been for a short or long time, when you decide to get back into the game, it's OK to wonder if there are any side effects from staying away from sex for so long. It is possible that you may feel anxious, and this can interfere with you enjoying sex again and the health benefits that come with it. This anxiety can even cause you to exhibit some sexual dysfunction symptoms like erectile dysfunction (ED) or premature ejaculation (PE).

Another angle not often considered is that if you have been finding other ways to pleasure yourself, such as masturbation, you may deal with desensitization of the penis, which can make it harder to ejaculate.

There are different side effects you can experience as a result of celibacy. Let's go through some of these side effects

- Anxiety

If it's been a while since you've been intimate with another person, it's very likely you'll deal with some sexual performance anxiety when your sex life heats back up. Sexual performance anxiety means that you may fear you wouldn't measure up during sex.

Fears that can pop up when you haven't been with someone for a long time can involve wondering if you'll be able to get an erection or if you still remember how to pleasure someone else or if your penis is big enough. This type of anxiety affects not only your mental health but your physical health. The physical effect includes erectile dysfunction and premature ejaculation.

Also, if one of the ways you've managed your abstinence period is by watching porn, it can explain why you would struggle with your sexual activity. Porn can actually cause anxiety that is because when you compare real-life experiences to what you see in porn, it can create feelings of inadequacy.

When you're anxious, the sympathetic nervous system is triggered, resulting in the constriction of your blood vessels and the release of the stress hormones epinephrine, norepinephrine, and cortisol, which all translates to you finding it a lot more challenging to keep an erection during sexual activity.

- Desensitization

Have you ever heard of the "death grip syndrome"?

If you've been masturbating too frequently as a way of dealing with your period of celibacy, you just might have the "death grip syndrome."

Not to worry; this isn't a medical term. It's just conversationally used to describe that if you often masturbate with an overly firm grip, it can result in a desensitization of the penis, further making it difficult for you to reach orgasm.

Now how can you treat these side effects?

If you're dealing with anxiety, it can very well go away on its own, especially after the first time you have sex again.

But if it doesn't go away, the following can help:

• ED Medication
Suppose you have begun having sex again and the feeling of anxiousness hasn't resolved and you still find it hard to get and maintain an erection. In that case, you may be experiencing erectile dysfunction. ED medication may help with getting a healthy erection.

These medications work by dilating blood vessels, which increases blood flow to the penis. There are a variety of prescriptions you can use, such as Viagra. You will need to consult and speak to your doctors about this to get a proper medication if this is the treatment you want to pursue.

• Premature and Delayed Ejaculation Treatments
Understandably, you may ejaculate early if it's been a while since you had sex. This anxiety isn't limited to males who have been celibate.

According to research, premature ejaculation fear appears to be linked to sexual performance anxiety. SSRIs, which are commonly used to treat depression, are one type of medicine used to treat PE.

Another way to manage this is to use an anesthetic cream or spray on the penis. These topical creams desensitize the penis, allowing you to go longer between ejaculations.

But what if you've already been desensitized to the point where you can't ejaculate? To allow your penis to become more sensitive again, you should stop masturbating. And even when you masturbate, use a softer grip

- Therapy

Talking to someone can help you learn to manage the anxiety that arises from celibacy. CBT (cognitive behavioral treatment) might be of help.

Your approach should be to talk to your therapist about what causes your anxiety in romantic relationships and intimacy and to come up with strategies to alleviate your anxieties.

You may be wondering what CBT is? It is founded on the premise that specific psychological issues are caused by unhelpful thought and behavioral patterns. When you engage with a CBT-trained therapist, they'll teach you how to spot distorted thinking and problem-solving skills to help you deal with challenging situations.

When You Don't Have Sex for a Long Time, Your Body Suffers

Regular sex, according to research, has plenty of health benefits for both older men and older women. These benefits are not gotten when you're celibate, benefits such as reduced blood pressure and less risk of issues with your cardiovascular system. These benefits include:

• Improved Immune System Function

Frequent sex helps your body fight against illness, so having it a reduced number of times often might lead to more colds. A recent study discovered that college students who had sex one to two times per week had higher levels of a specific antibody (called immunoglobulin A) that plays a vital role in the immune system.

• Lower Risk of Prostate Cancer

For men, the chances of prostate cancer can be linked to how often they have sex, but the evidence is mixed. A large study of almost 30,000 men showed that those who claimed they ejaculated more than twenty-one times a month on average had lower chances of prostate cancer during their lifetimes than those who ejaculated four to seven times a month.

Some other experts think that sex may raise your chances of having prostate cancer by exposing you to sexually transmitted diseases that lead to inflammation. It's essential that you protect yourself against sexually transmitted diseases by using protection if you have multiple sexual partners

• Reduced Anxiety and Stress

When you don't have sex with your partner frequently, you may feel less connected with them, which means you won't talk about your feelings as much or get a lot of support in handling your day-to-day stressors.

Sex causes your body to release hormones such as oxytocin and endorphins that help you manage the effects of this stress. Plus, oxytocin also enables you to sleep better.

- Memory

The research for this is still in the early stages; however, some studies have shown that people who have sex often can easily recall memories. And there are also signs that sex can help your brain grow neurons and even work better generally.

- Relationship Health

No matter your age, gender, or how long you have been with your partner, regular sex helps you feel emotionally connected and close to your partner. This opens the door to better communication and allows you and your partner to lead a happier life than those who get less of it. Strong pelvic floor muscles

- Vaginal Walls and Lubrication

If you've gone through menopause, it's an even more incentive to keep having sex. Without frequent intercourse, your vagina might tighten, and the tissues of your vagina can thin, making it more likely that bruising, tearing, or even bleeding will occur during sex.

This can be so painful that women who are experiencing these symptoms avoid having intercourse, which can worsen the problem.

Lubricants, moisturizers, and low-dose estrogen can be used to address menopause-related changes such vaginal dryness and discomfort.

Sex as a Longevity Block

Aging is a natural process change that occurs in the body over time. It is associated with different biological, physiological, environmental, psychological, behavioral, and social processes. As we age, we're naturally inclined to begin to look for ways to increase our lifespan. We want to look good and live long indeed; every adult aims for longevity. Research has shown different ways by which we can improve and elongate our lifespan. Some of which include our food, drugs, exposure to a toxin, sleep pattern. Ways we can improve our longevity include:

• Consuming a Nutritious and Well-Balanced Diet
Increase your life expectancy by consuming a nutritious and balanced diet. A suitable balance of the three macronutrients: proteins, fats, and carbs, should be included in your diet. Avoid consuming a lot of fattening or deep-fried meals. To receive the proper nutrients and vitamins, include plant-based foods like fruits, vegetables, nuts, and seeds in your meals.

Overeating and unhealthy late-night snacking should be avoided. A balanced diet is what you should aim for if you want to acquire the right nutrients from your food.

• Exercise on a Regular Basis
Another technique to lengthen your life is to exercise and stay active. Try to fit in cardio-based workouts like jogging, jumping rope, or boxing every day or on a regular basis. You may become physically active by exercising for at least fifteen minutes each day. If you can walk or bike to work, even your commute may be a good workout.

Spend a few minutes extending your legs or walking about if you spend most of your day cramped up in a small office or sitting down. Regular exercise is essential and making it a habit of it will help you achieve your goals.

- Avoid Common Vices

You will have a shorter life expectancy if you engage in common vices. Smoking has been linked to illnesses such as lung cancer and premature mortality. It is never too late to quit smoking if you are a smoker. While consuming alcohol occasionally or for special events is OK, excessive alcohol use is harmful to your pancreas and liver.

Take care not to take any dangerous medicines since they might negatively influence your health and well-being. Avoid engaging in vices since there are healthier alternatives to spend your leisure time.

- Stay Positive

According to studies, feeling well and being happy might help you live longer. Don't allow anxiety to overtake you by dwelling on the unpleasant aspects of life. Try to cheer yourself up by doing things you enjoy or by spending time with friends and family.

While this doesn't imply you should go through life clueless about what's going on around you, aiming for a cheerful attitude might help you feel better. If you spend the majority of your time worrying and fretting about everything, it will reduce your mood, make you feel unhealthy, and have a long-term detrimental influence on your body.

- Maintain a Healthy Sleeping Routine

Sleep is a crucial component in achieving your aim of living a long life. Having a disrupted sleep schedule or not receiving enough sleep on a daily basis can have a negative impact on your mood and health. For the rest of the day, you'll feel fatigued and irritable. You'll be unable to perform adequately due to a lack of energy.

Sleep should be a period for appropriate rest, with an average of eight hours suggested. Decent sleeping hours assist your body in growing taller as you get older; thus, having a good sleep schedule influences your height as well.

Asides from all these ways listed, one rarely-talked-about longevity block is sex. Sex is usually known for certain benefits such as stress relief, reduced pain, and even enhanced immunity. However, amongst all this is the fact that sex can actually make you look and be seven years younger. A new study by a clinical psychologist and former head of psychology at the Royal Edinburg Hospital, Dr. David Weeks, noted that having sex can make you look five to seven years longer. The study also showed that intercourse can expand your life expectancy.

My-mindguide.com

Chapter 3

How to Get an Older Woman in the Mood

Older women find sex more difficult because the body changes due to the drop in hormone levels. These changes make sex difficult and less pleasurable. Like I mentioned earlier, women experience vaginal dryness and thinning of the tissues during and after menopause. These changes make sexual activities difficult and can reduce their desire or interest to engage in any sexual activity.

In addition, the health issues, aches, pain that develop with age, and of course, child-bearing can take their toll, and others rescue their interest in sex. For example, many older women complain of back pain, affecting their sexual attraction. Women are also emotional beings, so they tend to feel less sexy as they age, disrupting their mental focus, confidence, and sexuality.

As an older man, you must take note of these changes and learn how to work with them. Don't be quick to dismiss your partner by saying she's not interested in sex; you have to get her in the mood to make the experience a seamless, painless, and enjoyable experience.

There are specific tips I'll be sharing with you that will help you get your partner in the mood and give both of you an enjoyable experience. These steps can and should be taken by both you and your partner.

TIP 1: COMMUNICATION

Communication has always been the key to a successful and long-term relationship. Communicating your needs and desires to your partner will give you satisfying sex. The physical and functional aspects of sex aren't rigid, and so you need to be ready to make adjustments because what was once pleasurable may not be again. It's essential for you also to have a non-judgmental conversation with your partner. Talk about the changes occurring in both your bodies, your changes in desires, and most importantly, listen and pay attention to your partner. This way, you are sure to navigate any problem that might arise.

TIP 2: DE-STRESS

Getting an older woman in the mood is tricky; you don't want to add stress to the situation. Stress is a major mood killer, so it's almost certain that she won't be interested in any form of sexual contact if she's stressed. It would distract you both and make it further impossible to build that sexual intimacy you desire. Therefore, take time for you both to relax; a bath, massage, and meditation can help you get in the mood for sexual activity.

TIP 3: ALWAYS USE LUBE

One major factor that always makes older women uninterested in sex is the dryness of their vagina. The decrease in estrogen associated with menopause causes a significant reduction in vaginal lubrication. Using lube is a straightforward solution to make sex more pleasurable and not painful. With lube, a normally hesitant older female will be open to having sex and would make the experience more memorable for you both.

TIP 4: SLOW AND STEADY

Besides dryness, there is also a reduced elasticity and decreased tissue density in the vulva and vagina. In addition to this, aging comes with less energy, easy fatigability, and more significant heart health concerns. All of this means that your sexual activity should be done slowly and carefully. Rushing your approach to sexual activity is what you want to avoid when getting your partner in the mood. Take plenty of time to arouse each other and enjoy the experience at a slower pace.

TIP 5: FOREPLAY

Don't neglect foreplay; it's a handy tool to get an older woman in the mood—in fact, any woman of any age. Foreplay is essential for both partners' arousal. You need to realize that sex isn't all about penetration, and a lot of pleasure and enjoyment of sex can come from the chase and tease. Insufficient foreplay is a primary reason women don't achieve orgasm or be sufficiently aroused for any pleasurable sexual activity.

TIP 6: CONSIDER USING TOYS

Incorporating sex toys into your sex life will help reduce getting in the mood. There are different types and versions of sex toys that are partner-friendly. With the number of online retailers available today, you don't have the excuse of embarrassment about going into a sex shop. Toys help alleviate any issues you might be experiencing in your sex life.

TIP 7: BE OPEN TO TRYING NEW THINGS

Combined with using new toys, trying new things is another excellent way to improve arousal and desire. Don't be shy about trying out new sex positions, kinks, fetishes, and role-playing scenarios. Explore and find something new that excites and gets you and your partner turned on and in the mood. Experiment and try out new things. As mentioned earlier, communicate with your partner about these new ideas. There's no limit to how much you can experience in the bedroom.

TIP 8: ROMANCE

Keep the romance alive in your relationship. Don't neglect it. Don't fall into the trap of seeing your sex drive and frequency drop simply because you and your partner have been together for a long time. Have regular date nights, and show each other love through acts of service. Let your partner always feel loved through the care and attention you show her.

TIP 9: PLAN AHEAD

As you get older spontaneous sex may not exactly work out. It's necessary to have a clear plan for your sexual activity. Set a time and work towards it. That way, limit any form of distraction. By doing this, you and your partner can have time to prepare and anticipate the sex, especially if you plan to try out a roleplaying situation.

TIP 10: SUPPLEMENTS AND MEDICATIONS CAN BE HELPFUL

If you tried out most of the tips I have given above and you and your partner still find it challenging to improve your desire and sexual function, you may consider supplements or medication. Sexual function issues can be treated and improved using prescription medication, over-the-counter medicines, and accessories. Talk to your doctor about the best options for you. Don't be shy; by asking questions, you'll be sure to get the answers and recommendations you desire. Also, if you have any health condition, your medication can be interfering with your sex life, so don't hesitate to clear that out with your doctor.

Sexual Positions That Make Things Easier

As you get older, new sex positions are something you have to consider. Your body is undergoing changes that could lead to back and knee pains. So if you're trying out sex and it's difficult for your body, a new position would make things easier, more comfortable, and more enjoyable.

As an older adult, the best sex positions for you are those that evenly distribute your weight over all your joints and, most significantly, reduce the strain on your back. During intercourse, old injuries and diseases such as arthritis might resurface. Aside from keeping to your most comfortable positions, you may need to strike a balance between changing things up frequently enough to be comfortable but not so frequently as to irritate your joints.

I've put together different sex positions that are appropriate for you; however, because every couple is different, you and your partner will need to try some of the various positions and then settle on the ones that work the best for you both.

- **Missionary:** This is a classic sex position that works for both the young and elderly. The bottom partner is fully supported from beneath, allowing the man's weight to be off his partner and making it easier to have comfortable thrusting. In this position, the man puts himself on top and rests his weight in an even manner between each of his forearms on either side of her. He also bends his knees and rests them on either side. The woman can also put her legs on her partner's lower legs to allow for more comfort. This position can easily be modified by placing a pillow underneath the hips of the partner on the bed.

- **Spooning:** Both partners lie on their sides, facing the same direction. The woman lays on one side, and the man cuddles up at her back using the same side of his body as hers. In this position, the man can easily penetrate the vagina without putting any extra pressure on his knees or arms. This position can easily be modified to make entry easier if the woman lifts her leg over her partner's. Each partner can control the rhythm of the sex, and placing pillows between the woman's legs or wedging cushions behind the man's back will help support the weight of their bodies. Spooning allows for a deeper connection, as partners can hold each other close while making love. It's also better for clitoral stimulation.

- **Chair Position:** A chair without armrests is used for this position. The chair should be slim and low enough for the two of them so they can comfortably touch the floor with their feet. The man sits down, and the woman sits on his lap, facing him. This position allows for easy penetration. The woman gives herself extra support by putting her hands on her partner's shoulder or on top of the chair's backrest and comfortably controls the motion's rhythm, depth, and speed.

This position is excellent for those who can comfortably straddle their partners.

- **Coital Alignment Technique:** The Coital Alignment Technique was created with the intention of providing more clitoral stimulation than the Missionary Technique. The male raises his hips over his partner's clitoris and rubs his pubic mound on his partner's clitoris. CAT may be a preferable senior sex position since it depends more on grinding.

- **Thigh Pillow:** This spin on sideways 69 could be the senior sex position you've been hunting for, especially if you're having trouble finding comfortable positions for delivering a blow job or receiving oral sex. To stimulate your spouse's genitals orally, line up head-to-toe with your partner. Your bodies are supported since you're on your sides. In Thigh Pillow, your top arm is free for increased manual stimulation!

- **Leg-over-Leg:** This may be the simplest of all the sex positions for seniors. You're both lying on your backs. The receiver drapes their closest leg over their partner's leg and rests a portion of her butt on her partner's hips. This allows penetration by aligning their genitals.

Now, although these conditions can limit and affect your sex life, there are adjustments you can make that, despite the medical issues, you can still have a satisfying sex life. Let's take a look at some of these conditions and positions you can assume.

- Arthritis causes joint pain that makes sex uncomfortable. You can consider the following sex positions:

- For men with back pain, a side-by-side position will work best. This position takes off the pressure on your back and joints. To achieve this position, you and your partner will lie facing each other with your legs intertwined.

- For a woman with hip arthritis, lying at the edge of the bed with the partner either standing or kneeling in front of her is a more comfortable position. The partner straddling him on top for a man with knee arthritis is a more comfortable position.

- Stroke: A side-by-side position will be ideal. Also, a position with the affected man's partner on top would work as well.

Sex Is Not Just Intercourse

Most of us make one misconception: that sex without intercourse is not sex. Assuming that only intercourse constitutes absolute sex limits our expression, creativity, and satisfaction. Let us get this out of the way: sex without intercourse is still sex.

Many older women are seen to define sex as vaginal intercourse, which may be seen to influence the decline in sexual activity, especially if the male partner is less healthy and unavailable.

The truth is that sex is any activity that arouses you and brings you sexual pleasure.

Below are simple reasons why your need to see beyond intercourse:

- Erection tends to weaken with age, so if you limit sex to penetration, you're bound to have less sex.

- Performance anxiety also kills erection. With age, you can be concerned that your erection is hard enough—a natural mood killer.

- Specific medical issues, as previously noted, can make intercourse impossible, so you have to switch to a different kind of sex, or you won't have any at all.

- Your skin is extremely sensitive. It's a *wonderland* of sensation. For this reason, there is no limit to the pleasure you can feel once you look past intercourse.

- For many women, as they age, penetration becomes uncomfortable and even painful such that even with plenty of lubricants, long intercourse can still be awkward.

- Most women, about 75 percent, don't attain orgasms solely through intercourse, and with age, the percentage gets higher. The clitoris, not the vagina, is pleasant for most women. Even though many women find intercourse fascinating and pleasurable, they still require clitoral stimulation; for some, the leading form of sex is clitoral pleasure.

- When men rely on erectile performance drugs (e.g., Viagra), it only gives them an erection, not libido, so although they get erections, it may still take them longer to reach orgasm, which can be uncomfortable and painful for them and the female partners alike.

These issues point to one thing: older people should concentrate on what brings the most amazing sensation. Take the focus off intercourse and focus on goal-free success and pleasure.

Sex without Penetration: What to Do Instead

Now that we know that penetration is not the alpha and omega of the sexual experience, let go of that notion and stop ignoring other ways to please yourself. Let's expand our practices and ideas to all the different ways we can arouse each other, share intimacy, and enjoy orgasms.

There are so many options; some you might find are for you, and others might not attract you. There's no wrong way for sexual expression if it's enjoyable and consensual. Learn, experiment, and decide on your ways.

Here are some non-intercourse ways to enjoy sex:

- Like I mentioned earlier, the skin is the largest sex organ, so feel free to explore each other's entire bodies. Let your partner touch your body all over, and you, too, switch to exploring your partner. There's plenty to discover about the body, how it looks and responds. Do this whether or not you've known each other for a long time or just a little while.

- Sensual full-body massages never go wrong. Take plenty of time to give your partner a massage using different massage oils with fragrances. Your goal here is to provide your partner with relaxing pleasure. Take note of the moans, the sighs, and your partner's breathing pattern. This will help you know you're doing the right things and help you build arousal and even bring about an orgasm.

- Erogenous zones are your friend. Erogenous zones can change with age. Explore these new zones; that way, you can find what turns you on. The way you can discover this is by touching new spots and gauging the response, whether with your partner or solo. Actively seek the areas that are arousing for you and your partner.

- There are different ways to touch—lighter or harder, direct or teasing, faster or slower. Sometimes getting aroused is less about where you feel but about *how* you feel. Communicate with your partner about what speed works. As you get prompted, what excites you may change. There's no right or wrong way to enjoy touching. Communicate with your partner about what excites you when you're starting, when you're aroused, and when you're close to orgasm

- Your mouth is a beautiful tool. All genders find the warmth and pressure of the mouth alongside the movement of the tongue very enjoyable. Oral sex never goes wrong as long as you're doing it the right way. Also, note that oral sex doesn't have to be just foreplay; it can be the main event.

- Use sex toys. A well-designed vibrator can give you the intensity you require for orgasm. There are also sex toys available for the penis, which are just as important and pleasurable.

- Self-pleasuring together can be very intimate and satisfying. Here, you pleasure yourself, and your partner does the same with you, either watching each other simultaneously or taking turns. Masturbating together can be a valuable tool to teach each other how you like to be pleasured.

- Let go of any goals you had in mind and focus on pleasure. As sex and relationship coach Charlie Glickman, Ph.D., puts it, *"Sex is a lot like a buffet. We have so many different choices for pleasure and intimacy. Intercourse is a popular dish, and it's a favorite for many people. But there's no reason to skip past all the other options or consider them only as appetizers. When you do that, you miss out on discovering lots of other delicious possibilities!"*

Remember to take your time. You're learning new skills; plus your arousal is slower than it used to be. Be patient with yourself and your partner.

Getting Comfortable

- Touch a lot during non-sexual times. Sit close to each other, hold hands and reclaim the awareness of how good your body feels when they're close and not having sex.

- Take time to look into each other's eyes. Try to remove the awareness from yourself and focus on your partner.

- Kissing and making out stimulates the brain and increases the sex drive. Spend lots of time kissing, and it doesn't have to lead up to sex. Try relaxing into your kissing and breathe in sync.

If you've been in a relationship that's been entirely focused on intercourse, follow the steps below to initiate the switch. Creating the button without a gradual process can be awkward.

- Have an honest conversation about the importance of exploring the other different ways of achieving physical intimacy. Listen to your partner without any interruptions.

- You can have sexual encounters that are entirely devoid of intercourse. Here, you will explore how to give your partner pleasure, and then you'll be the one receiving pleasure. Ensure you give each other plenty of feedback at the moment about what feels good using your words, moans, and gestures.

- Talk later about the experience, how it can get better and what you would like to try next.

Communication is key. It cannot be overemphasized, as it's the bedrock of sexual intimacy. Learn to communicate.

Why Do You Need to Talk About Your Sexual Needs?
In a recent study by Bob Eren, it was seen that nearly 60 percent of older people are unhappy with their sex life. The big reason? They weren't talking about it. On the other hand, it was seen that those who had support from others, including their doctors and their spouses, were much more likely to be sexually active and sexually satisfied.

You need to know that, in life, the more we talk about most things, the easier it gets. This applies very much to sex—something alone that carries much stigma, alone adding the invisibility of older adults having sex. Moreover, it's essential that you ask others for help, especially if physical ailment, a sense of isolation, or something about your environment keeps you from having the sex life you want. You don't need to feel shameful about being vocal about your sexual health as it's a vital part of your physical, mental, and even spiritual health.

Here are some ideas for getting started if you're of a specific age and want to reconnect with your sexuality or just pay more attention to your sex life:

- Talk to your doctor

You may feel that your sex life is a low priority, especially if you have a lot of other health issues to deal with, so it might not be worth bringing up at your next doctor's appointment. But the fact is that your doctor is highly familiar with your medical condition and can make precise suggestions for improving your capacity to have sex, whether that means prescription drugs or altering your health plan to keep your sexual functions thriving. Don't hesitate to talk to your doctor.

- Look for a sex therapist or other professionals who work with people in your age bracket.

If talking to your primary care physician doesn't seem right or is not yielding many results, you can consider seeing a sex therapist or another expert who can help you feel comfortable and safe addressing your sexual desires. You might be surprised by the range of services available out there—sex coaches, sex educators, tantra instructors, sexual healers, doulas, and various other specialists can all help you navigate this area of your life.

- Talk to your friends and romantic partner about sex.

Communicating about sex with your spouse and others may lead to a more fulfilling and satisfying sex life. If you have a sexual partner right now—even if it's someone you've been with for decades—discuss how they feel about your sex life right now and whether they'd be interested in reprioritizing it with you. Open up and tell them about what you've been thinking about, the health advantages, and how you'd like to go back into this field.

Also, discussing sex with your friends has been proven to boost sexual confidence and self-efficacy. As you develop confidence in discussing this personal aspect of your life, you'll find it simpler to talk about your wants and ask for what you want.

- Find a retreat or a community that can help you explore
If you don't have any close friends with whom you'd like to discuss this, look for open-minded groups of individuals in your age group with whom you can have more conversations about sex. Retreats and seminars on intimacy may be a fantastic opportunity to learn, reconnect as a couple, and meet others who are on the same path. (If you or your partner are uncomfortable, ashamed, or timid about the concept of sexual exploration, these sorts of gatherings can be an extremely warm and approachable setting to help you expand your mind, become more comfortable, and let go of some of your fears.) If you're unsure whether events are appropriate for you, you can always contact the organizer to learn more about the target age groups.

The Internet is also an excellent resource for finding such communities in your city. Google around or post in social media spaces where you're comfortable. You can also try asking people in your age group to see what resources they are aware of.

- Read, Read and Read

Just like this eBook, other excellent reading resources can give you endless ideas, resources, and inspiration about exploring your sexuality at your age.

- Expand your definition of what sex is.

This is very important because as we get older, certain types of sex that may have been exciting in the past are less doable, but it doesn't imply that all sex should now be off the table. Consider trying different sorts of sexual expression and activities if. In the past, sex involved a lot of thrusting and acrobatics, concentrate solely on giving and receiving pleasure with your hands, arms, and tongues, for example. There are still plenty of sexual acts that will provide those wonderful neurochemical pleasures. Cuddling, for instance, is linked to increased sexual pleasure and satisfaction, as the brain itself can function as a sex organ. Reading, viewing, and writing erotica can help boost sexual arousal as well.

There are a variety of ways to experience love, intimacy, and pleasure, both alone and with a partner, that have nothing to do with penetrative sex. Look for something that suits your personality, talents, and interests.

How to Get Better Sex

Sex can be a negotiation, especially with a new partner. Learn to ask and study your partner to know what they like, what you need to do for them to reach orgasm, what makes them uncomfortable, what are they willing to try, what's essential, and what's off-limits

Check out which of these approaches fit your style.

"Could we try . . .?"
"I'd love it if you'd touch me this way."
"Show me what feels good to you."
"What would you like?"
"Show me how you pleasure yourself."

If you and your partner are new to each other, you'll need to think about a few more things. What method will you use to bring up your sexual wants and restrictions, and when will you do so? How and when do you mention that intercourse will be difficult or impossible?

I recommend bringing it up as soon as you notice that the relationship is heading in the direction of sex.

Rather than framing your need or desire for sex without penetration as a low restriction or an apology, word it positively, using phrases like these:

"I'm drawn to you. Although I'm unable to engage in sexual activity, I would like to explore all of the other ways we may enjoy each other."

"I'm looking forward to seeing where this goes."

"I'm drawn to you. Although I can't engage in sexual activity, I would like to explore all of the other ways we can enjoy each other."

"I'm looking forward to seeing where this goes. Is it possible to investigate how to make love to each other without the intention of intercourse?"

"I'm afraid I'll have to tell you that we might not be able to have sexual relations. However, if you appreciate it, I'd be delighted to fulfill you with my mouth and fingers."

OLD
IS
NEW
BLACK
My-mindguide.com

Chapter 4

Self-Love

What Is Self-Love?

Self-love means different things to different people because we all have different ways to care for ourselves. Fundamentally, self-love is a state of appreciating yourself, and this appreciation grows from actions that support your psychological and spiritual growth. When you love yourself, it means that you have a high regard for your own happiness and well-being. You take care of your own needs and do not sacrifice your well-being to please others. Self-love means you don't settle for less than you deserve. By understanding what self-love is, you would be able to practice it.

Figuring out what self-love means for you as an individual is a very important part of your mental health. So let's break it down.

What does self-love mean to you?
Self-love can mean different things. For starters, it can mean:

- Talking to and about yourself with love
- Prioritizing yourself

- Giving yourself a break from self-judgment
- Trusting yourself
- Being true to yourself
- Being nice to yourself
- Setting healthy boundaries
- Forgiving yourself when you aren't being true or nice to yourself

Self-care is another method of expressing self-love. You frequently need to do the following in order to exercise self-care:

- Pay attention to your body
- Take pauses from work to stretch and move
- Set your phone aside, connect with yourself or others, and/ or do something creative
- Eat healthy while indulging in your favorite meals on occasion.

Self-love means accepting yourself for who you are in this moment. It means accepting everything that you are, your emotions for what they are, and overall putting your physical, emotional, and mental well-being first.

How and Why You Should Practice Self-Love
Now you know that self-love motivates you to make healthy life choices. When you value yourself highly, you're more likely to make decisions that benefit your health and well-being. These things might include eating well, exercising regularly, and maintaining good relationships.

There are several ways you can practice self-love. They include:

1. Being more mindful: when you have self-love, you know what you think, feel, and want. You will be focused on your needs, not wants. When you take actions based on what you need, you tend to steer away from automatic behavior patterns that keep you stuck in the past and reduce your self-love.

2. Practicing good self-care: Taking good care of your basic needs allows you to love yourself more. A representation that you are high in self-love is that you enrich yourself every day through healthy activities such as exercise, good sleep, good nutrition, healthy social interactions, and intimacy.

3. Creating space for healthy habits: To truly care for yourself, you have to start showing it in what you eat, what exercise you carry out, and what you spend your time doing. It's important that you do stuff because you care about yourself, not just because you have to or need to get it done.

4. Be kind, compassionate, and gentle with yourself just the way you would with any other person you care about.

Here are some tips if you want to strengthen your self-love:

• Practice Mindfulness and Self-Compassion
You can practice mindfulness and compassion by meditating. Meditate when you are feeling overwhelmed. This helps you

practice living in the moment. Whatever you feel, acknowledge and accept the reality, take care of what you are feeling, and nourish it with self-care. Give yourself the freedom to embrace what you feel in the moment.

• Daily Affirmations

We easily compliment our friends and even strangers, but we become hard on ourselves when it comes to us. So, from this day onward start to say something nice to yourself—things like: "I am loved," "I am enough," "My past experiences do not define me," and many more. You can find words of affirmation online and even from listening to music.

• Self-care

Self-care refers to how we look after our mental, emotional, and physical well-being. Recognizing and embracing your emotional condition, getting adequate sleep, eating healthy, utilizing body and skincare, exercising, forgiving yourself, taking time for yourself, and confronting bad ideas are some ways you can express self-love.

Take a few days to pamper yourself in the midst of your hectic schedule. Make an effort to do something that makes you joyful. It might be anything:

• Getting up in the morning
• Relaxing in a hot tub
• Eating breakfast with your favorite foods
• Shopping
• Reading a book
• Binge-watching movies

- Anything else

Below are a couple of activities you can do in your day-to-day life to promote self-love:

- Do something you enjoy or something that you are good at. It will cause your body to release endorphins, making you feel happy.

- Allow yourself to be pampered/nurtured with a nice relaxing bath or a body massage. You've earned the right to be the finest version of yourself

- Accept yourself for the good, the terrible, the ugly, the sexy, and the stinky. Accept yourself as a whole individual.

- Cook yourself delicious meals with all the necessary veggies and fruits.

Can it Help to Forgive Ourselves and Our Adversaries?
When was the last time you truly accepted and welcomed your feelings?

When was the last time you didn't blame yourself for everything that went wrong due to circumstances you had no control over?

When was the last time you looked in the mirror and congratulated yourself for getting this far?

I'm almost certain that it's either been a long time or you haven't done so at all. So, before you continue reading this book, I want you to do the following:

Look at your reflection in the mirror, put your hands on your chest and say the following words genuinely:

"Thank you. Thank you _______ (insert your name here) for putting in such a good effort and trying this hard. Thank you for not giving up despite having hundreds of reasons to do so. I'm so proud of you. You did great for standing until the end. It's OK if you've made some mistakes because no one is perfect. I forgive you, and I love you".

One common mistake we make is comparison. We compare how we feel with the appearance of our friends. We always worry about what other people think about us. We often do not feel enough about our appearance, weight, skin conditions, and so many things we consider as flaws, especially as we grow older. We find it the hardest to accept ourselves because we tend to want to be perfect.

However, these imperfections are what make us different and special, right? These imperfections in ourselves that we can't fix might be the one thing that sets us apart makes us different and even more attractive to others.

My dear reader, the truth is just as you love others, you need to love yourself. You are someone you should treat with love, kindness, and compassion. Stop the blame game! Stop blaming yourself because something didn't go as planned, stop blaming yourself in the mirror because you don't feel good enough, and please don't compare yourself to someone you see on social media. The only person who has the right to compare you to who you were in the past is yourself. The key is to become better versions of ourselves in the present, and that's enough. Don't be too harsh on yourself; the world is hard enough already.

The first sign of self-love is forgiveness. Forgiving is the highest and purest form of love. When you forgive others, you receive the ability to forgive and love yourself. It's OK not to have learned all this in the first twenty or thirty or even fifty years of our lives; the important thing is to start now. Self-love and forgiveness are in a loop. When we learn to forgive ourselves and others, it becomes easier to attain self-love, and the more we attain self-love, the easier it is to forgive.

Self-forgiveness starts with you reflecting on past events from a different angle.

Many people hold themselves responsible for their past decisions and actions. If you feel the same way, remember that you don't have to since you change through time and your previous decisions were the best you could conceive of at the time. You may now forgive yourself for not knowing better in all of those previous circumstances. You would have made different choices, said different things, and done differently if you had known better. Allowing yourself to forgive releases a great deal of energy and helps you accept and love yourself more.

Everything will start falling into place after you've decided to let self-forgiveness into your life, and you'll see yourself take the first step toward more self-love and self-acceptance. You won't be able to fully accept yourself if you try to love yourself while holding grievances against yourself.

Say these words with me:
I forgive myself
for having made mistakes.
Had I known better,
I would have chosen differently.
So, I forgive myself.

Forgiveness and self-love give us spiritual and emotional healing. If we can forgive people, we can rid our hearts and souls of all grudges against them and fill them with love and compassion. Grudges towards people have just one effect: they harm our spiritual health and well-being. The following are some of the advantages of forgiving someone in your life:

- You will have unlimited happiness in your life.
- It liberates you from all forms of hatred and jealousy.
- Others will become more forgiving of you,
- You will become more open toward others.
- It will teach you patience to endure other people's actions.
- Your connections and relationships will become stronger and deeper,
- It will boost your confidence and self-esteem.

Our longing for self-love is deeply rooted in our ability to forgive others. Think about this deeply:

How can you learn to love yourself while others accuse you of being selfish and irresponsible?

How can you learn to love yourself if your surroundings are dark and gloomy?

Remember, when you love yourself, you accept yourself as you are. You honor your feelings and respect your limitations. Prioritize your happiness and health because if you don't love and forgive yourself, you won't be able to truly love and forgive others.

There will always be criticism and bad remarks that might drag you down, and everything you do will always appear incorrect to some people. However, dear reader, you were not created to be flawless, and it isn't your responsibility to meet everyone's expectations. You were created to be you, and you are the only one in the world. Whatever others may say about you will not define you or determine your fate.

So, what should you do?
Let yourself rest.
Let yourself not be perfect.
Let yourself make some mistakes.
Let yourself feel broken.
Let yourself be happy, sad, or angry.

Then,
forgive yourself.
Forgive yourself for not being strong enough.
Forgive yourself for all the mistakes that you have made in the past. Your past is a part of you that you need to accept and forgive.

Forgive yourself and then rise again.
You are not alone in this journey, and even I am on a journey to loving myself. It's not easy, and there are so many struggling

too. Self-love is a lifelong process, and I'm so glad that you're starting this journey now. There's nothing like being too old; you still have a long, fulfilling life ahead of you.

Remember, unlike what society tries to portray, self-love isn't about your looks. As you get older, your body begins to change, which can affect how you feel about yourself and your sexuality.

Once you start living from a place of inner power, based on self-love and self-forgiveness, you change from a position where the world used to force its laws on you, prompting you to seek external acceptance, permission, and reassurance. You enter a place where the world caters to your wants and supplies you with everything you require to continue unfolding. It all begins with a simple, heartfelt willingness to let more love and forgiveness into your life:

"I am willing to accept more love and forgiveness into my life."

When you start changing, your relationships will begin to transform. You will watch your relationships blossom, your intimacy begins to grow, and then your sexual desires become more attainable. What no longer serves you will be allowed to fade away. Because you've learned to love yourself, you'll be able to engage in current relationships from a new point of inner strength, making them more rewarding and empowering for everyone involved. Amazing circumstances will offer you fresh contacts with whom you will be able to open yourself in a different way.

By just implementing some of the steps and behaviors I have listed above, You will ultimately grow to love and respect yourself more than anything else in the world. And if you allow yourself to do these things, you will find it easier to forgive people and encourage more self-love inside yourself and with others.

It's time to finally be your best.

The Concept of Hypnotherapy and How It Can Help Improve Your Sex Life

Hypnotherapy, also known as hypnosis, is a therapeutic technique that produces an altered state of consciousness in the person by inducing deep relaxation. Hypnosis puts you into a trance-like state in which you have heightened focus and concentration. It's usually done with the help of a therapist using mental images and verbal repetition. While in this state, the therapist makes suggestions for behavioral changes. When you are under hypnosis, you will feel calm, relaxed, and more open to suggestions.

Hypnotherapy, an alternative form of therapy, is often used alongside cognitive behavior therapy and medication.

Choosing to undergo the process of hypnotherapy is a completely voluntary act. As a patient, you are always in control of your actions and can withdraw when you want to. The hypnotherapist cannot make a patient do anything they don't want to do. Hypnotherapy is only performed by certified mental health professionals who are specially trained for this type of therapy.

How Does Hypnotherapy Work?

There are four main stages of hypnotherapy. I will take you through these four stages, so you know what to expect.

The first step is **Induction.**

The hypnotherapist uses several techniques to induce hypnosis in the person. The individual is taken through four steps. The hypnotist tells the person to:

- Close their eyes.
- Imagine that they can't open their eyes.
- Try to open their eyes while pretending they can't.
- Relax the eyes and the whole body.

There are different techniques the hypnotist uses to induce a person

- Eye-Fixation Technique

This technique involves focusing the gaze on a certain item until the eyelids grow heavy and close, and the person relaxes deeply.

- Arm-Drop Technique

The person focuses their sight on one of their fingers while keeping their forearm vertical until the hand gets heavy and begins to fall downward. The eyes get heavy and close as the arm lowers, and hypnosis is accomplished.

- Progressive Relaxation Technique

The person sits comfortably, concentrates on inhaling and exhaling, and relaxes their entire body from the feet up to achieve full relaxation.

- Imagery

Imagery entails the person inhaling deeply and seeing a situation that makes them feel safe and secure.

The second step is to deepen the hypnosis.

After inducing the hypnosis, the hypnotherapist deepens the hypnotic level because an individual is more likely to respond more positively in such a state. Some of the techniques applied during the induction phase may be used in addition to the following:

- Progressive relaxation
- Visual imagery
- Periods of silence
- Deep breathing and counting
- Counting

The third step is Posthypnotic suggestions.

In this stage, the individual is already in a deep hypnotic state, so the hypnotherapist begins to make suggestions to counter problems with behavior or stop addictive habits like smoking or alter the response to pain symptoms. They also ask the individual leading questions to induce the person to talk about deep-rooted trauma, after which appropriate therapy is provided.

Termination is the last stage.

The most common way a hypnotic state is terminated is by counting from one to five or five to one.

Hypnotherapy, Intimacy, and Sex

Sexual intimacy with our partners, especially as we age, is an important part of a fulfilling relationship. When we have these sexual issues, it can lead to tension and difficulties whether or not we're in a relationship.

When it comes to sexual problems, Hypnotherapy helps you understand that the root of the problem you are facing may be associated with stress and anxiety. It then helps you rebuild confidence.

If you discover that you have sex-related problems, consulting your doctor is the first step because it may be that an underlying physical condition associated with aging may be causing the problem.

An interesting thing to note is that there's a psychological element at work for a lot of these problems. This element could be stress, anxiety, low self-esteem, and even past experiences you had when you were younger. The goal of hypnotherapy is to help you identify the root cause and change your thinking of the problem.

Your hypnotherapist using positive suggestions can help to reduce the associated stress and anxiety around sex by suggesting a more positive approach for you.

Common examples of problems men face include premature ejaculation, erection problems, loss of libido, inability to reach orgasm during sex, and dyspareunia (pain during sex).

What Sexual Problems Can Hypnotherapy Help With?

There are a variety of issues that hypnotherapy may help with, and here we'll look at some of the more frequent ones that men may have.

- Premature Ejaculation

Premature ejaculation is a familiar term, and it is used when a person ejaculates too quickly during sex. However, this "too quickly" varies from person to person. The NHS did a study that considered the average time taken to ejaculate for 500 couples from different countries of the world. This time was found to be about five minutes. There is actually no correct duration when it comes to sex. It is up to you and your partner to decide.

There are two types of premature ejaculation: Primary premature ejaculation, where this has always been a problem, and secondary premature ejaculation, where the problem recently developed. As an older adult, you are more likely to have a secondary premature ejaculation.

After your doctor has ruled out any medical causes, you must investigate physical, psychological, or a combination of both causes. Depression, stress, relationship troubles, and anxiety about sexual performance are all common psychological factors.

Hypnotherapy uses the power of suggestion to encourage good changes on a subconscious level. Because stress and worry can often contribute to premature ejaculation, hypnotherapy for stress and anxiety can be very beneficial. Other benefits of hypnotherapy include increased self-confidence and self-esteem and visualization.

I don't know how to act my age.
I've never been this age before
My-mindguide.com

- Loss of Libido

As we age, both men and women may suffer a decrease in sex drive. It's frequently connected to stress, exhaustion, or even relationship problems. Everyone's sex drive is different, but if yours is exceptionally low and causing issues in your relationship, you should get help.

Seeing a doctor will help you rule out any physical issues (such as hormone problems or a side-effect from medication). They can also assist you in determining the source of the problem and suggest treatment to help you and your spouse reclaim a satisfying sexual life. Hypnotherapy can be a useful tool for some people.

Hypnotherapy can assist with sex drive issues in a variety of ways. If stress, worry, and/or depression are to blame, hypnotherapy geared to these issues could be helpful. Lack of confidence and self-worth can influence libido in some people, and this is another area where hypnotherapy can help.

- Erection problems

It is very common for men to frequently struggle to obtain and maintain an erection. Alcohol consumption, stress, and exhaustion are common reasons that don't cause alarm. However, if your problems become more frequent, you should consult your doctor.

Erection issues (also known as erectile dysfunction or impotence) can be caused by physical or psychological factors, similar to premature ejaculation. If you only have erection issues sometimes (for example, if you can get erections in the morning but not during sex), it's possible that you're suffering from a psychological condition.

Erection issues can also be caused by mental health illnesses such as depression and anxiety, and your doctor may prescribe therapy if this is the case.

Sex therapy may be recommended, especially if you believe your relationship is suffering. Another alternative is hypnotherapy, which may assist with tension and anxiety as well as confidence.

When it comes to erection issues, stress and performance anxiety can be major concerns, and hypnotherapy can help. A hypnotherapist can help you better respond to stress and lessen anxiety by effecting change on a subconscious level.

Hypnotherapy aids in the natural processing of negative ideas and events, transforming them from flashbacks to narrative memories that no longer trigger a stress reaction.

- Anorgasmia

Anorgasmia, also known as *orgasmic dysfunction*, occurs when a person is unable to achieve orgasm during intercourse. Both men and women can suffer from this. However, it is thought to be more frequent among women.

There are a variety of reasons why people fail to achieve orgasm, ranging from medical ailments to psychological and emotional issues. Seeing your doctor can help you figure out what's causing your symptoms. There is a multitude of therapeutic methods available, including hypnosis, for this and other sexual disorders.

Anorgasmia might be triggered by bad memories and expectations from previous sexual encounters. Hypnotherapy can aid in the improvement of self-esteem and the re-patterning of negative sexual connections.

Anorgasmia can lead to ideas such as "I can't get an orgasm," and hypnotherapy can help you shift those beliefs that are holding you back. Because stress and anxiety often contribute to anorgasmia, hypnosis for stress and hypnotherapy for anxiety can be beneficial.

- Dyspareunia

When you have dyspareunia, you get pain during intercourse. Dyspareunia is more frequent in women, although it can equally affect men. During (or after) intercourse, men may experience discomfort in the genital or pelvic region. During or after ejaculation, some men may also experience a burning sensation.

Both physical and psychological factors can cause pain during sex, so see your doctor rule out any medical issues. Stress, a history of sexual abuse or trauma, sex anxiety, and depression are all common psychological factors.

In terms of treatment, sex therapy may be suggested, and hypnosis for pain can be useful in some circumstances.

It's understandable to be anxious about sex if you find it to be an unpleasant experience. Hypnotherapy can help you overcome your fears and boost your confidence. Hypnotherapy for pain relief aims to alter your pain-related thinking processes, resulting in a significant shift in your pain perception.

Sex Therapy vs. Sexual Hypnotherapy vs. Erotic Hypnotherapy

Sex therapy is very different from sexual hypnotherapy and erotic hypnotherapy. In sex therapy, the therapist offers psychosexual therapy by using talk therapy to get you to understand the problem you have. They usually work with you and your partner in a session offer ideas for activities and projects you can try at home to get things to improve. The aim here is to help you and your partner be more open to confronting the problems you face and finding a way to overcome them.

On the other hand, hypnotherapy (either sexual or erotic) for sexual problems focuses more on helping you make changes deep in your subconscious. Here, there are fewer discussions. The hypnotherapist will induce you into a state of hypnosis where they then offer positive suggestions.

If you've tried sex therapy but the problem is still persisting, this could mean that you need a change at the subconscious level.

Sexual Hypnotherapy: How Can It Help?

Talking about sex issues can be difficult and embarrassing for a lot of people, especially as you get old; it gets increasingly difficult to discuss this issue. As a result of this, most people may refrain from seeking help. But staying silent can only make the matter worse and can lead to a lot of stress and unhappiness in your life and that of your partner and even those around you.

Normally sex therapy is usually most effective when and successful when both partners are involved. At times, it can be difficult to get your partner to show up, especially if they feel they aren't the problem. This is the advantage sexual hypnotherapy has over sex therapy in that it can be used to treat an individual without involving the partner. When your sexual problem has an emotional cause, hypnotherapy is the best way to understand and overcome the problem.

Hypnosis uses techniques that allow quick identification of underlying conflicts, unresolved feelings about past events, and factors beyond your conscious awareness. Below, I will show you the ways hypnotherapy can help you overcome any sexual problems you may be facing

- Positive Thoughts Towards Sex

You and your therapist, through hypnotherapy, will work on your subconscious mind, which stores all of your memories and monitors all of your bodily functions to unmask the root cause of your problem. By using regression techniques, you'll be able to heal all past trauma you may have experienced and remove any anxiety you have toward sex.

The hypnotherapist also provides positive suggestions that make it easy for you to focus on pleasurable thoughts and feelings about sex to aid you in having a healthy sex life. Neuro-linguistic programming (NLP), for example, is a method that can assist in re-alignment of your mind and removing any self-imposed 'blockages.' If you're suffering from anorgasmia, for example, your hypnotherapist can help you maintain an open mind and a good attitude so that intercourse can naturally develop to orgasm.

- Visualization

Using visualization techniques will allow you to start seeing yourself in a new light. You begin to see yourself how you want to be or how you want to achieve a specific goal. Affirmations also aid in reinforcing the image you are focusing your mind on.

So, for example, if you are having body images issues or you're struggling with your partner seeing you naked, which isn't unexpected since you're getting older and your body is changing, you can work with an affirmation that says, "My partner sees me as sexually attractive." By the continuous practice of these techniques, even outside of your hypnotherapy sessions, there will be an increase in your chances of success. You can request recordings of the sessions from your hypnotherapist, which will help you with these affirmations.

- Reduce Stress

Stress is one thing that can affect every area of your life, especially your libido. When we're stressed, hormones are released as a natural response to how we are feeling, so this is what can impact your sex drive.

We know, of course, that it's impossible for us to remove all forms and sources of stress from our lives; however, what we can do is to change our response to them. Hypnotherapy helps with this by helping you to identify specific causes of stress, anxiety, and worry in your life, then help you to develop the techniques to control these feelings

- Promote Relaxation

In a relaxed state, your mind is better able to accept and adapt to the suggestions that your hypnotherapist is making. So, your hypnotherapist ensures that the environment for your session is calm and helps you concentrate on your breathing so that your body can relax easily and get back into synchrony. The goal here is to allow your mind to focus.

With the help of hypnotherapy, you will start to feel confident and more relaxed, thereby allowing your body to enjoy a sexual and intimate relationship that feels great.

Erotic Hypnosis

Erotic hypnosis is also referred to as hypno-sex and can be used to elicit pleasure. However, this pleasure doesn't just refer to orgasms. Erotic hypnosis is simply the use of hypnosis to create or attain a specific sexual goal in some shape or form. This sexual goal can be a hands-free orgasm or a relaxing and pleasurable state of mind. Here, one person guides the other person into a trance-like state by using only their voice and then suggests certain behaviors and attitudes.

Erotic hypnosis is a way of heightening or enhancing the things that a person already enjoys. It can pull things out that would have otherwise remained hidden, thereby making the person more sensitive with a lowered inhibition if that's what wants to be achieved. Here, sexuality is played out in an indirect way.

There are so many reasons for you to practice erotic hypnosis. Some of these reasons include:

- Increase awareness of one's sense of touch, sensations, and thought processes
- Control pleasure during and/or after trance

- Induce hands-free orgasms
- Enhance role-play and fantasy
- Experience something that seems to be a "taboo."
- Transform a kink or fetish
- Let go and relax

How Does Erotic Hypnosis Work?

At the beginning of every session, your hypnotist lays the foundation, which involves talking about your goal for the session, your soft limits and hard limits, and insights into your life. It is necessary they have this information because the more pieces of the puzzle they have, the better it is.

Every laying the foundation, the hypnotist induces you into a trance. In this state, your attention leaves the immediate environment and fixates on your inner experiences such as feelings, cognition, and imagery.

We experience various light trances at least twice a day in our daily lives—trances like when we wake up and tick off our list of to-dos or when we reflect on our day before sleeping or even when we zone out when driving and miss our exit. So, when under hypnosis, you enter a consciously-induced trance that mirrors these lighter trances you already experience daily.

Everybody's experience of their induced trance differs; how you experience yours depends solely on the suggestions made by your hypnotist. Your relaxed state of mind can resemble drowsiness, sleepiness, floating, or fuzziness. Everyone has a unique hypnotic experience. Some people get exceedingly calm, some get turned on, while others remain completely unaffected.

You would remain in that very deep state of relaxation until the session is over or if something snaps you out of it.

You may be worried that you won't do something against your core values because your inhibitions are down. However, this is untrue because although your inhibitions are lowered, you don't lose control of your morals or who you are as a person. A good example is that if you're an animal lover and your hypnotist makes a suggestion that you should run over an animal, you will snap awake because the suggestion isn't who you are. The whole process is voluntary and will only leave you feeling lighter than you were before.

Hypnosis Orgasms

It's possible to have orgasms during erotic hypnosis, which is sometimes referred to as a *hypnosis orgasm*. However, you shouldn't go into your first session with the aim of having a mind-blowing orgasm. It's actually quite hard to attain in your first session. Having a hypno-orgasm is an eye-opening experience. It makes you realize that the largest sex organ is actually your brain.

Your body takes the record and remembers everything you've ever felt, so erotic hypnosis lets you experience these inner sensations by engaging your mind.

How to Try Erotic Hypnosis

1. Find a hypnotist you can trust
Carry out your research to find out what you want out of a session. Then, look for hypnotists that have credentials, prior

clients, references, and a website. This research is very important because not everyone who practices this erotic hypnosis has the best intention. There is a fine line between hypnosis and brainwashing, so be careful of hypnotists that tell you to only be "beholden to them only" outside of your already-agreed-upon power play. How the hypnotist phrases the suggestions is critical to guarantee a safe session, so any suggestions that go against your moral values should be objected to outright.

2. Determine how you want your session to go
When you have found a hypnotist, decide if you want a physical session or an online session. Another option is to listen to prerecorded audio files. Even if your session isn't physical, you can still have a great connection through personalization, as hypnosis is very much about rapport.

3. Manage your expectations
Trance happens in levels, and a level of deep trance may or may not happen. A lot of confusion that occurs with hypnosis happens when the person leaves the session with no recollection of what they did. Therefore, it's expedient that you have a good grip of what you expect a successful session to feel like. You should know how to gauge whether a trance is deep enough to feel like you've achieved something. Go in with a reasonable expectation and an open mind because if you're consciously resisting it, then it's unlikely to work.

4. Don't get discouraged
People's experiences vary; some are able to fall asleep immediately, while for others, it can take hours. There are different reasons that can prevent you from entering that

deep state of relaxation. Reasons like not being able to let go or not giving your hypnotist enough information about you leave them unable to make suggestions. It's OK to have an unsuccessful session, so don't get discouraged if you do not get it on your first try.

5. It's OK to be skeptical after the session

Speaking from experience, the natural desire to test a suggestion is natural. It's OK to want to test it out for yourself to see if these suggestions have brought about any real change in your sexual life.

What Are the Risks of Hypnotherapy?
The main issue with hypnotherapy is that it may be impossible for certain persons to achieve hypnosis. Although adverse effects to hypnotherapy are uncommon, some people may experience the following:

Headache
Drowsiness
Dizziness
Anxiety or discomfort
Irrational thinking (creation of false memories)

Abreaction: emotional outburst as a result of recalling prior trauma (this may be utilized as a part of the therapy)

Sex Toys and Sexual aids for Older Adults

Why Should Older adults Use Sex Toys and Sexual Aids?
In this age and time, the use of sex toys has become increasingly acceptable. Many people now realize that these toys only help

and add to the enjoyment and pleasure of sex. I strongly believe older adults shouldn't be left out from enjoying the pleasure that sex toys bring, which is why I have added this section.

Sex toys are made to stimulate the most enjoyable parts of your body. This includes the clitoris, vulva, G-spot, and prostate. They are called toys for a reason: they make your sex life and relationship more enjoyable, fun, and playful. They allow you to discover what feels nice, add diversity to your sexual activity, and allow you to experiment with new sensations. Vibrators and sex toys are excellent for older adults because:

- Women's arousal time tends to rise as they become older.
- To attain orgasm, you need a longer arousal time.
- After strong, repeated actions, arthritic wrists, knuckles, and other joints might get weary.
- Sex toys can go into areas and handle situations that you might not be able to.
- Even if you don't have a companion, you should "enjoy your own company."
- Sex toys can assist in alleviating some of the physical symptoms of aging.
- They're a lot of fun and nothing like they used to be!

What Sex Toys and Sexual Aids Work Best for Older Adults?
Not all sex toys and sexual aids are made the same. Likewise, everyone is different and so would like different sex toys. There are cheap sex toys, and there are high-quality sex toys.

As an older adult, it is important that you take a lot of factors into consideration when buying a sex toy. For example, strength is an important factor when choosing a sex toy—the reason being that as a woman ages, blood flow to the genitals is reduced, meaning that there is less sensitivity and it takes longer for her to get aroused. The vaginal area also becomes more sensitive, so sex toys that are made of soft materials such as silicone will be gentler and feel better on the body.

Partners can go for a couple's vibrator or other sex toy that will help both partners feel pleasure during sex. For example, a vibrating penis ring would turn an erect penis into a vibrator and also constrict blood flow from the penis, leading to a harder and longer-lasting erection.

So, luxury vibrators for older adults are better than the cheap ones because they:

- Are powerful for long periods of time.
- Are easy to use with easy-to-find buttons.
- Are easy to hold but not too heavy.
- Are rechargeable.
- Are soft.
- Are the right size for internal stimulation, especially for those who experience vaginal soreness and decreased elasticity
- Are FUN!

How Can You Get Started with Sex Toys and Sexual Aids?
If you've never used a sex toy before and you're wondering where to start, there are certain questions you need to ask yourself.

As an older man:
1. What should it look like? Do you want a cock ring or a vibrating pouch? Do you want something less conspicuous that doesn't look like a sex toy?

2. Do you have any movement restrictions or physical issues? What position would you be in when using it?

3. How do you want it to feel against your skin? There are different shapes and sizes of sex toys (e.g., flexible, hard, soft, smooth, or textured).

4. Will you be traveling with the toy? You might want to consider going with one that has a travel lock feature.

As an older woman:

1. How do you want to use your vibrator? Do you want a vibrator for internal stimulation of your G-spot, or do you want one for the external stimulation of your clitoris? Do you want a vibrator that will stimulate you both externally and internally at the same time? Do you want to use it for masturbation or with your partner during sex?

2. What should it look like? Do you want a sex toy that looks like a penis? Do you want something less conspicuous that doesn't look like a sex toy?

3. What size are you looking at? This is important because a size that would have seemed perfect years ago may be too big and uncomfortable for you to know, especially if your frequency of penetrative sex is irregular.

4. How do you want it to feel against your skin? There are different shapes and sizes of vibrators, such as flexible, hard, soft, smooth, or textured.

5. Will you be traveling with the toy? You might want to consider going with one that has a travel lock feature.

What If You Don't Like a Toy After the First Time You Use It?
Before passing judgment on the toy, give it at least 3–4 attempts. When you do anything new for the first time, you are more focused on the novelty and perhaps discomfort of the scenario. Your body is unfamiliar with the sensation, and your mind may wander.

It's also vital to keep in mind that everyone is unique and has a unique body. What works for one person might not work for another. So, there is no such thing as the "greatest" toy; there is only the best toy for YOU!

Everyone deserves a respectful and satisfying sex life, and this feeling doesn't fade with age. While there have been numerous design-forward sex toys on the market, many of which may be considered by individuals of any age, there are several considerations that people may need to make as they get older, including, but not limited to:

- Maintaining arousal and reaching an orgasm is difficult.
- Ergonomics (using a product that is easy to hold and operate).

While there aren't many toys marketed exclusively to older adults, there are a number of products already on the market that can solve some of the issues that you may face.

Since it can all get a bit confusing, I've curated and grouped the sex toys into three categories: sex toys for older men, sex toys for older women, and sex toys for couples. These toys can all be purchased on Amazon.

SEX TOYS YOU CAN TRY OUT AS AN OLDER ADULT FOR OLDER MEN

1. Colorpop OWow Vibrating Ring

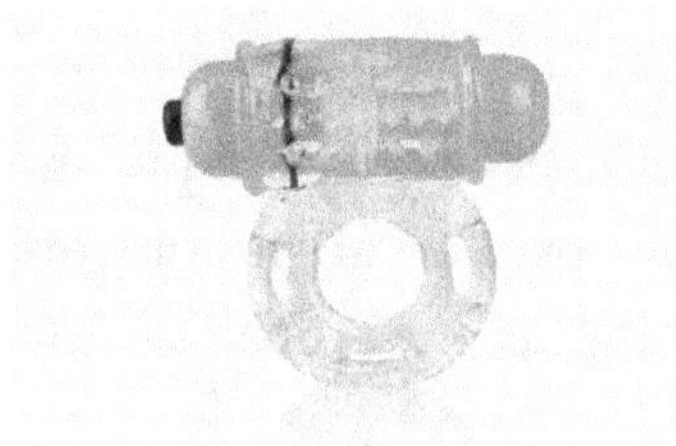

A vibrating cock ring is a good option if you're searching for something simpler. It allows blood to flow into the penis rather than out, and it can help you sustain a stronger, longer-lasting erection. However, you can also use it on a dildo to provide vibration to the person who is being penetrated, or even just on your fingers to act as a non-slip vibrator. If you don't want to spend a lot of money, a vibrating cock ring is also a good option.

2. We-Vibe Pivot

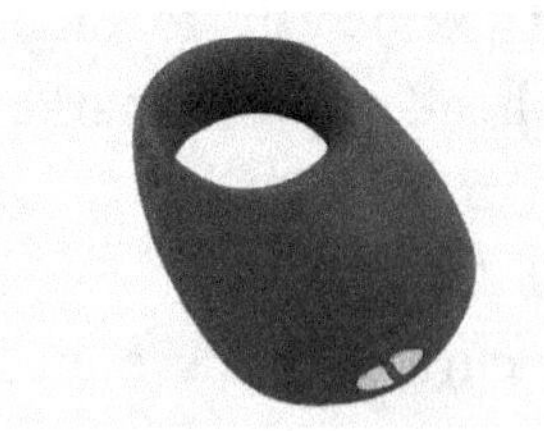

WeVibe's Pivot is also fantastic since it can be used for two purposes. Because of its powerful vibrations, you might just use it as a clitoral vibrator. Instead of putting it on a penis during penetration, you could just hold it in your hand and place it over your partner's clitoris during intercourse.

3. Hot Octopuss Atom Vibrating Ring

The Atom, a wonderful penis ring from Hot Octopuss, is also available. This one, like the Pivot, is really strong. The vibrations may be felt throughout the ring. The Atom, on the other hand, has a larger contact surface, which is intended to make it as comfortable for the person rubbing up against it as it is for the one wearing it. There's also the Atom Plus, with the size of the ring being the major difference between the two. The ordinary Atom is meant to sit at the base of the penis shaft; however, the Atom Plus is large enough to glide over both the shaft and the balls for perineum stimulation.

4. Ohnut Intimate Wearable Ring

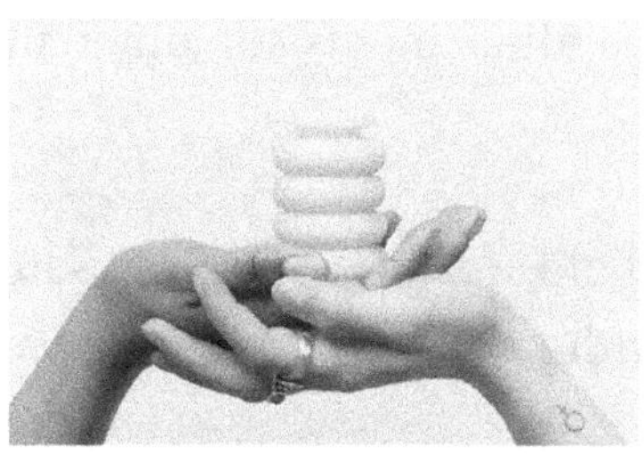

If you're someone who deals with vaginal pain during sex, the Ohnut, a series of interlocking silicone rings, can really help. You can put it on a penis or on a toy, and it controls the depth of penetration. it can also work well for people experimenting with anal play who want to start with shallow penetration before working up the full length of a penis or a toy. Then you can remove one of the rings and it's like half of the penis or toy is entering. It's been found to be a really great couples toy.

FOR OLDER WOMEN

5. Le Wand Petite Massager

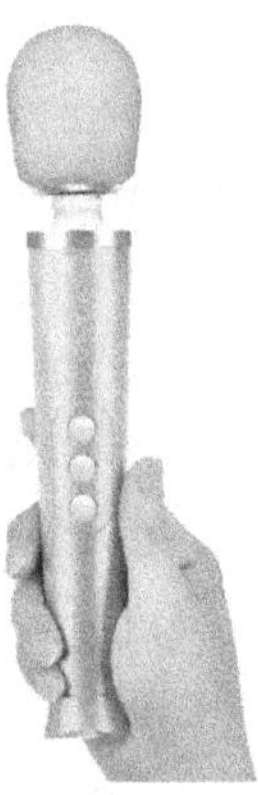

This is a rechargeable massager that is easy to hold and powerful especially if you're dealing with arthritis. Aside from the soft silicone on its head, it has various attachments for different sensations.

It is powerful, small, easy to hold, featuring a body-safe silicone head and flexible neck, with simple controls that are ideal for beginners

6. Dame Fin Finger Vibrator

Fin is little but strong, and it's simple to put on and take off. This vibrator mimics your hand's natural movement and acts as an extension of your hand, delivering stimulation wherever you want it.

It's ergonomic and simple to operate, making it perfect for those with disabilities and individuals who have a difficult time gripping a vibrator. It's an excellent toy because it is strong, easy to hold, and easy to use. Moreover, it's small, can be used with or without a tether strap, and is rechargeable, making it a great toy for beginners.

7. OhMiBod Lovelife Cuddle G-SPOT VIBRATOR

OhMiBod The Lovelife Cuddle is a top-selling luxury vibrator with a unique G-spot stimulation curve.

With its delicate curvature, which is required to stimulate the G-spot, the Lovelife Cuddle G-spot Vibrator was specifically designed for G-spot stimulation. The ridged tip of the Cuddle helps to increase the pressure that your G-spot demands. Cuddle is designed for G-spot stimulation, but it may also be used externally.

8. Tenga Iroha Mikazuki and Minamo Internal Vibrators

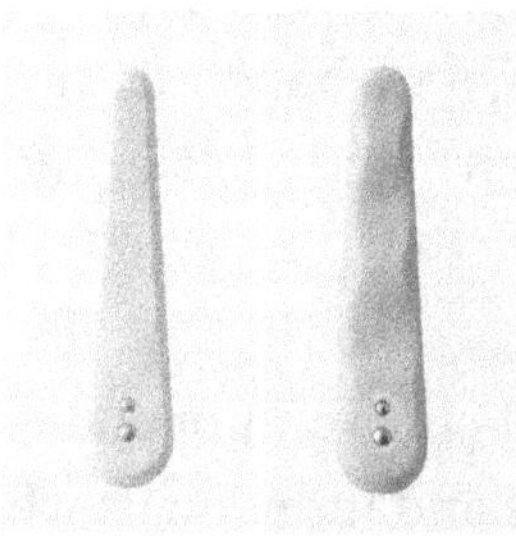

Internal vibrators Tenga Iroha Mikazuki and Minamo are thin. If you don't have penetrative sex on a regular basis, these subtle vibrators are ideal, as they feature gentle to moderate vibrations that are cushiony, not rough.

Iroha Mikazuki grows in diameter from .7 inches to 1.1 inches in the middle and then to 1.4 inches at the end. Iroha Minamo, on the other hand, grows from .9 to 1.3 inches.

Why is it a great senior sex toy?
- Powerful
- It's simple to hold
- Adaptable (allowing users to reach all the right places)
- Controls that are simple to use
- Gentle to moderate vibrations

FOR COUPLES

9. Eva 2 by Dame Products Hands-Free Couples Vibrator

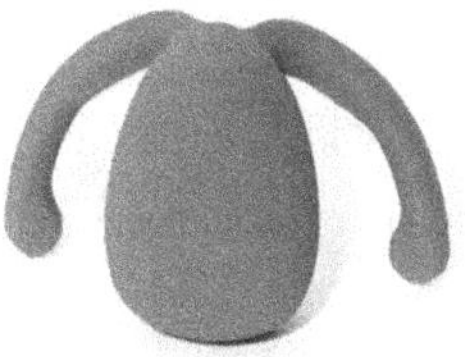

The Eva 2 is a gentle, hands-free luxury vibrator that is ideal for older women. Because of its flexible wings, this fantastic sex toy may be used alone or with your partner and will stay in position pleasantly.

Because it's hands-free, it can be worn during penetrative sex, stays in place, and is powerful, this unit makes a great senior sex toy.

10. We-Vibe Melt Stimulator

Try the We-Vibe Melt if you want a toy for partner sex that allows both participants to climax. Without overstimulation or the need to stop, gentle suction and airwaves stimulate the clitoris.

The thin, curved shape is lightweight and comfortable to grip. In whatever sexual position, it fits wonderfully between you and your lover.

It's a great senior sex toy since it's easy to grip, fits comfortably between two people during sex, and is great when both lovers want to have fun.

Best Sexual Stimulants for Seniors

Sexual stimulants contain physiologically active substances that have a physiological impact. People can use them for pleasure, to try something new, or to be really helpful, depending on the sort of influence the product has.

Arousal products, libido boosters, and desensitizers are the most prevalent stimulants.

FOR PENISES

Rise Stimulating Gel by Sliquid Ride

Ride Rise Stim Gel is a male sexual stimulant that improves penile sensitivity for increased sexual satisfaction.

With peppermint oil and menthol, which are natural vasodilators, this sexual stimulant softly stimulates blood flow to the surface. Instead of using L-arginine, a common irritant found in other stimulation gels, this unique composition relies on plant-based and organic botanicals to soothe and thrill sensitive skin. As a consequence, guys may use a natural and healthy arousal gel alone or with their companions.

FOR VULVAS
ON Arousal Oil

ON Clitoral Arousal Oil is a popular all-natural female stimulant that increases orgasm and feeling during sex.

It is completely natural: This clitoral stimulant, made with a special combination of essential oils and botanicals including sweet almond oil and *Cinnamomum cassia* to generate a safe, natural arousal impact unlike any other, is shockingly potent.

It gets the job done quickly. Unlike other stimulating gels and oils, ON Clitoral Arousal Oil produces an instant warming feeling on the clitoris, followed by a buzzing, vibrating, and throbbing sensation. This mixture stimulates nerve endings and boosts blood flow, resulting in a more intense sensation with each contact. Most significantly, ON's clitoral stimulant makes it simpler for women to experience orgasm. ON Arousal Oil helps a woman's body respond more quickly to physical stimulation and provides her with the sort of full-body awareness that boosts her arousal level. These two factors make it simpler for women to experience orgasm.

Natura lubrication is increased: Another advantage of ON Arousal Oil is that it may really assist some ladies in increasing their own lubricant production. This might be especially beneficial for women experiencing hormonal changes, undergoing a hysterectomy, or taking drugs that reduce their body's capacity to self-lubricate.

It's so effective as a sexual stimulant because:
- It's for ladies who want their orgasms to be more intense or faster.
- It's perfect for dry-skinned women or those going through menopause.
- It promotes lubrication, according to many women.
- It's ideal for ladies who have dry skin or are going through menopause.
- Many women claim that it improves their lubrication.

Destined
to be
an old woman
with no regrets
My-mindguide.com

Exploring Sexuality After Sixty

Many people who have taken after the twentieth-century school of thought believe that sexuality and all the aspects of sexual expressions were reserved for the young. Although the earliest form of research believes that sexual interest can continue well into one's fifties, sixties, and seventies, there are many limitations in those studies. Still, when the topic was looked at in a broader sense, it was revealed that sexual expression was more apparent in older people who had active sex lives when they were younger.

To an extent, this conclusion was true, but the entirety of an older person's sex life couldn't be judged whether or not that person had an active sex life. There had to be more consideration to conclude why the older generation didn't have an active sex life. As a result of studies and societal norms, older people are relegated so much so that it is not believed that a 60-year-old woman or man is sexually active anymore. So, movies like *Dirty Grandpa* and other Hollywood portrayals of people well above sixty with active sex lives are classified as raunchy and generally inappropriate. What this does is break the older generation from the possibility of sexual expression;

since society doesn't believe that they should be having sex at that age, they then follow suit. Consequently, marriages aren't the same anymore because the older that couples become, the less expressive they become sexually; why? Society frowns upon it.

Thankfully, the world we live in today has evolved tremendously; there is a firm acceptance of different things that were frowned upon before. Homosexuality is now a celebrated phenomenon, with people over sixty living their best lives with their partners. With society being open to certain sexual practices, older people have now become open about their sexual tendencies and express themselves more.

They Always Had a Naughty Side!

People above the age of sixty don't just happen to embrace their kinky side all of a sudden when they grow older, contrary to popular opinion. But the kinky side had always been there; it just needed some form of expression. This can be from the reciprocated love and affection of the spouse that allows the kinky side to blossom. There's no way that anyone, whether young or old, who has a kinky side can flourish with a pattern that doesn't accommodate such behavior. Therefore, there has to be a mutual understanding of the sexual expressions of both parties.

According to research, as we age, it becomes harder to have sex due to the changes in our bodies. The vagina walls become thinner and stiffer for women. Some women may have a hard time self-lubricating as they get older. For men, erectile dysfunction can be an issue as they get older, with difficulty sustaining an erection. With these complications, how does the older generation express themselves sexually?

This is where the entirety of sexuality comes to play; research shows that categorizing old people as "asexual" is based on an incomplete understanding of what sexuality means. The sexual expression doesn't necessarily mean that they are having regular intercourse. This might seem quite bizarre, but sexuality in itself doesn't only mean sexual intercourse, but sexuality encompasses the feelings, thoughts, and behaviors that you have for someone else. It's not only streamlined to intercourse. Therefore, for many older people, the pleasure isn't in the deed itself, but the satisfaction is in the intimacy, desire, compatibility, and mutual understanding of both partners. For many people, it's not about the intercourse but the feeling of trust and security when they're kissed or when their hands are held. The intimate behaviors that showcase deep emotions and affection are areas of sexuality that the older generation explores.

As an Older Adult, What Can You Do Going Forward?

First and foremost, accept and celebrate who you are!

The reality Is that sex in your later life may not be as it was when you were younger, but this doesn't mean it has to be wrong. Here's a chance for you to have more enjoyable sex than ever. When you embrace your older self, you can:

- Enjoy the benefits of the experience: There is independence and self-confidence that comes with aging which can be very attractive to your spouse or potential partners. Regardless of your gender, you may feel better at 65 or 75 than you did at

24. You may also know more about yourself and what keeps you excited and happy. Your self-love and experience can make your sex life more fulfilling for you and your partner.

- Look ahead and focus on other things: As you grow older, begin to let go of expectations you had of yr sex life. Try hard to avoid dwelling on the difference you can now see if you had sex actively in your younger years; there is n reason for you to slow down now unless you want to. Having a positive attitude and open mind would go a long way to improving your sex life as you age.

- Appreciate and love your older self: Your body is going to change as you age. You will look and feel differently than when you were younger. But by accepting these changes as natural and holding your head up high, you will feel better and even be more attractive to others. Confidence and honesty are two qualities known to gain the respect of others; they can also be sexy and appealing.

Restarting Your Sex Drive

Some older adults are seen to give up on having a sex life because of the medical and emotional challenges they face. However, most of these issues aren't permanent. You *can* restart your sex drive and get your sex life back on track. Maintaining an active sex life into your senior years is a matter of good health. Think about and become conscious of the fact that sex is something that can keep you in shape physically and mentally.

However, the road to this satisfying and enjoyable sex isn't always smooth. Specific problems can arise, and the first practical step is to find a solution to these problems.

Simply "do it." Sex is just as beneficial and vital as exercise, and it may provide you with pleasure and fulfillment even if you aren't "in the mood." So get back into the best habit of all. You'll start to feel better once you get into your rhythm, and your sex drive should automatically grow.

Increase your amount of physical exercise: Increasing your overall activity level will help your sex drive by giving you more energy and a better sense of well-being.

Use your age and expertise to be sensible and honest with yourself as much as possible. As you become older, let go of your emotions of inadequacy and allow yourself to enjoy sex.

If you enjoyed this title and would like to read about other topics that have changed my life, please check out my new books on Amazon or my website:
www.my-mindguide.com.

Also, let's stay connected on social media. Please drop a line on Facebook or Instagram, and stay tuned for updates! You're welcome to share your thoughts with me directly as well: gassner@my-mindguide.com. In return, I'll send you a gorgeous infographic that you can cut out and frame.

Also, please leave a review on Amazon, as this will help me to reach an even broader audience. Thank you so much for your time, insight, and undying hunger for knowledge!

I want to say thank you to all of my colleagues, clients, friends, and family members, who have all contributed to what I am now.

I also want to say thank you to Gabriel Palacios, the king of hypnotherapy and a Swiss bestseller author who taught this old fox new tricks, letting me deep-dive into the mystery of hypnotherapy. I learned so much along the journey that I'm now a certified master-hypnosis coach and conversation coach myself!

Furthermore, I want to say thank you to the fantastic teachers of SAMYANA/Bali who trained me to become a certified yoga and meditation teacher.

Last but not least, I give a special thanks to my master-teacher Eckhard Wunderle, who's close to a saint to me. He introduced me to the world of meditation and let me discover all the wonders it has to offer. I couldn't be prouder about having received my certification as a meditation teacher directly from him at the Institut für Spirituelle Psychologie.

Peace, love, and happiness to all of you—till next time!

Authors portrait

Kurt Friedrich Gassner has worn many hats throughout his lifetime, including but not limited to serial entrepreneur, Creative Director, Meditation Teacher, Licensed Hypnotherapist, and more recently, self-improvement author. Leveraging his treasure trove of experiences and in-depth knowledge of psychology, he provides his readers with the tools they need to unlock their infinite potential.

As a prolific self-help writer, Kurt has authored the following books: *The Art of Forgiveness, Lie or Die, Soul-Match, Can You Inherit a Poisoned Mind?* and *The Power of Poverty*. He also authored a best-selling children's book in German-speaking countries and has over 20 books underway.

When it comes to enduring success, Kurt understands that financial prosperity isn't the only aspect one should strive for. He may be a self-made millionaire, but what really transformed his life is mastering his unconscious mind. Perseverance, personal power, self-awareness, and learning from past mistakes have all been key ingredients to bringing his dreams to fruition—and he strives to impart that wisdom onto others through his writing.

During his spare time, Kurt Friedrich Gassner is either traveling across the globe, golfing, biking in the Alps, hiking, or spending quality time with his loved ones. For the last 37 years, he has been happily married and he is the father of two successful children. Presently, he resides in both Munich, Germany, and Kirchberg, Austria.

OTHER BOOKS BY THE AUTHOR

BÜCHER VOM AUTOR IN DEUTSCHER AUSGABE

BESTSELLING AUTHOR OF
The Art Of
FORGIVNESS
AMAZON #1 BESTSELLER
My-mindguide.com
A practical guide for self healing and overcome past traumas
The Art Of FORGIVNESS
KURT GASSNER
The Art Of FORGIVNESS
KURT GASSNER